THE SPORTING
Parent

Everything you need to ensure
your child succeeds in sport and in life!

Nathan Parnham

© Nathan Parnham
Edited by John Coomer.
Designed and typeset by WorkingType Studio.

The moral rights of the author have been asserted. All rights reserved. No part of this publication may be reproduced, stored in or introduced into a retrieval system or transmitted in any form or by any means (electronic, mechanical, photocopying, recording or otherwise) without the prior written permission of the copyright owner of this book.

1st edition, 2021.

ISBN: 978-0-646-83415-3

10% of the royalties on all book sales will be donated to various pathways for Australian sporting youth.

This book is dedicated to my parents Anne and Mark. Their tireless investments of love, patience and support has enabled me to wake up every day following my passion.

To my beautiful Nina, your unwavering peace, calm and guidance keeps me centred. I couldn't have achieved all of this without you.

*To my son Axel, you give me joy in waking every day.
May you find happiness in all that you do in life.*

About the Author

Nathan Parnham is a strength and conditioning specialist based in Brisbane, Australia. His career spans over 17 years, including a significant amount of time spent in the development/youth setting before he eventually transitioned into the professional arena. He has worked across a variety of sports with both genders.

His time in the development setting involved establishing athletic development programs in both government (Westfields Sports High School) and private school settings (Newington College/St Augustine's College/Brisbane Grammar School). He also contracted his services to various organisations during this time. Many athletes he worked with in the developmental setting have moved on to great heights, playing professional sport both within Australia and internationally.

Nathan has also displayed his versatility in the professional arena in a variety of sports with both genders. From the Parramatta Eels in the NRL through to the Australian Women's Sevens team.

The postponement of the 2020 Tokyo Olympics proved a pivotal point in Nathan's career. In the midst of the coronavirus (COVID-19) pandemic and on JobKeeper like many other Australians, he was provided with the opportunity to return to his true passion. Shaping our youth of the future!

With a new family of his own, Nathan took a step forward and never looked back. *The Sporting Parent* was born. His goal is to share the lessons he has learnt throughout his career on how to set your child up for success not only in sport, but in life! The outcome is a no-holds-barred 'go to' manual to help parents navigate their way through the confusing world of kids' sport.

Foreword by Darren Burgess

(High Performance Manager at Melbourne Football Club and formerly at Arsenal, Port Adelaide and Liverpool Football Clubs, as well as the Football Federation of Australia)

I first met Nathan in 2000. I was lecturing at Australian Catholic University in exercise science and he was a fresh-faced, first year student. He had an intensity about him that struck me immediately. When I put a note up outside my office asking for volunteers to help with a research project, it didn't surprise me that his was the first name to appear on the sheet. The project involved filming soccer and AFL players during games and involved late night, weekend work. While most 20-years-olds were exploring Sydney pubs and clubs at that time, Nathan was filming for a research project that offered him no personal benefit other than the experience. I knew he would make a successful career for himself in athletic development/sports science from then on.

During his 'uni' years, Nathan demonstrated a passion for helping, not instructing. He probably didn't know the difference back then, but there is one, and it's substantial. In some elite environments you can get away with instructing. Some professional athletes crave it, but kids need helping. They need guidance and empathy. Nathan offers both of those in spades.

It's no surprise to me that most of Nathan's career has been spent working with kids and adolescents in the long-term athlete development (LTAD) pathway. While some of his peers chased careers with elite sporting teams, Nathan has predominantly chosen the less glamorous, less financially rewarding path of working with kids and adolescents. He's dabbled in adult environments, and unsurprisingly was successful at both national (Parramatta Eels, NRL) and international (Rugby Australia, Women's Sevens) levels, but I suspect the call back to his true LTAD passion was too strong each time.

My PhD involved a commentary on what was missing in the talent pathway of Australian team sport adolescents. My conclusion was that we needed more people like Nathan — people who put the kids first, people who know the difference between longevity in the sport and winning on the weekend. People, like Nathan, who want to help. There are too many coaches and too many parents whose only focus is the upcoming game or the upcoming training session — they don't see the bigger picture. The sad reality is that for every Tiger Woods or Lionel Messi (who each dedicated themselves to one sport from the time they were toddlers through to adolescence), there are thousands of kids who have trained as hard, if not harder, and either didn't make it or gave up early due to burn out. You don't hear about the kids that dropped out.

That's where this book, and Nathan, come in. Kids today have more opportunities to excel in sport than they ever have. There are elite academies, private schools, sporting schools, personal trainers, fitness coaches and parents all competing (mostly with the very best of intentions) to assist kids to realise their full sporting potential. The problem is no one is talking to each other, and crucially, no one is talking to parents. Nathan and the contributors in this book have one goal — to provide you with the very best advice for your sporting child. They don't want your registration fees or your tuition money, nor do they want to claim any success stories because they coached 'Superstar Athlete

Foreword by Darren Burgess

A' when she was 8. They want to answer your questions and help inform your decision-making with your kids.

I know my Harry (10) and Millie (9) will be following Nathan's (and this book's) advice. Let Nathan and his contributors help your kids too. As a sporting parent I can assure you that both you and your child will be in the very best of hands if you do.

Preface

This is a book that had to happen! With close to two decades of experience in the combined developmental and professional sporting arenas, I felt obliged to write it.

To all the sporting parents out there, I applaud you. Firstly, for driving week in and week out to various sporting fixtures across the country. In many instances, for two or three of your kids. Secondly, for making the time to read this book. You're not only taking the time to educate yourself, but by the end of the book you will have empowered yourself to make informed decisions that will help your child succeed not only in sport, but in life!

The term 'sporting parent' has had a negative connotation for too long. It immediately paints the picture of enraged parents turning up ready for battle at their child's weekend sporting fixture. Forget the sport played, the time of year or seasonal variations — white line fever is often real and scary to some extent for the average Australian parent.

But what's wrong with wanting the best for your child if you go about it the right way? Nothing I say! Isn't that what every parent strives for when signing their child up for the various sports on offer throughout Australia? If you're not striving to provide every opportunity for your child to succeed (and most importantly, to enjoy the benefits of sport along their journey), then what are you hoping for?

If you agree with me, great! This is the first of many parts of your journey. But at times, you may find yourself frustrated, and even pissed off by what you read in this book. But I'm giving you unbiased information in absence of a personal agenda or financial gain.

Understanding the Game

Where do you start? How do you know where to find quality and reliable information? What products are likely to help your child succeed in their sporting endeavours?

To help you understand the answers to these important questions, I have divided this book into three parts:

Part 1 — How We Have Failed a Generation

Part 2 — Building the Foundations

Part 3 — Working Towards a Brighter Future.

Part 1 — How We Have Failed a Generation

It only seems like yesterday that kids' curfews in Australia were when the streetlights came on. All your mates in the street were beneficiaries of sporting birthday and Christmas presents — whether it was a footy, soccer ball, cricket bat or a netball. Many local telephone poles in Australia were transformed into basketball hoops. Makeshift skateboarding ramps collated from local building site off-cuts were the norm, as was the practice of boosting the smallest kid over a neighbour's fence to retrieve many a stray ball!

Sadly, that doesn't happen anywhere near as often anymore, and we as parents are largely to blame. The worst part is that it's adversely affected the development of fundamental movement skills in our kids. I explain how it has in Part 1.

Part 2 — Building the Foundations

Armed with the knowledge of how you can improve from Part 1, Part 2 will send you on your mission! Building the foundations provides you with the tools to set your child up for success. It is a one-stop shop. Your 'go to' source to overcome the 'I'd love to know how, but where do I start?' question!

Part 3 — Working Towards a Brighter Future

Once you've laid the foundations and you have your plan in place, how do you just be a parent? This might not be a book on how to be the ultimate parent, but it will provide you with the opportunity to implement strategies to increase the likelihood of your child's success. Does that translate to being a better parent? I'll let you decide...

Each Part of the book also has two special features — *Lessons from the Field* and *Think Boxes*.

Lessons from the Field

To enhance your experience, I thought it might be best to learn from the frontline. This includes parents who were once just like you, along with players, coaches and current practitioners in the field. This ensures that the book doesn't just reflect my coaching opinion, but rather a community to help, motivate and inspire you to be the best version of yourself as a sporting parent. These **Lessons from the Field** excerpts provide opportunities for you to learn from others who have done it successfully and/or who are paving the way for the generation of future stars to come.

Think Boxes

It's easy to read a book from cover to cover. But how many times have you read a book and really digested all the elements of it? Sure, you may remember a distinct section, or highlight paragraphs or ideas that grab you along the way. But if we truly want to digest the information presented, testing our understanding of it is the only way. These **Think Boxes** will help you to do that. Each one provides you with a moment to pause, reflect how the content applies to you, and whether you would make the same decisions again moving forward.

Not only is sport a journey through your child's development, but with this book you as a sporting parent too can grow as a part of that development! Be an active participant in the process — this is an opportunity where you have everything to gain and nothing to lose!

Understanding your role as a sporting parent and the impact of your decisions will not only help you make better decisions in future, but increase your child's likelihood of success. It's often when we stop, reflect and evaluate our own actions as sporting parents that we are empowered to become better people and parents along the way.

Contents

About the Author 1
Foreword by Darren Burgess 3
Preface 7
Understanding the Game 9

Part 1 — How We Have Failed a Generation 15
Chapter 1 Every weekend in Australia 17
Chapter 2 Work, life, balance 28
Chapter 3 Technology 33
Chapter 4 Fundamental movement skills 41
Chapter 5 Taking ownership 52

Part 2 — Building the Foundations 57
Chapter 6 Specialisation 59
Chapter 7 Sport selection 70
Chapter 8 Elite academies 86
Chapter 9 Understanding the hierarchy of schools, institutes and sporting bodies 92
Chapter 10 The elephant in the room (children and resistance training) 110
Chapter 11 Supplement use 123

| Chapter 12 | What does development/maturation mean? | 136 |
| Chapter 13 | Injuries and what they truly mean | 148 |

Part 3 — Working Towards a Brighter Future — 161

Chapter 14	Building resilient youth	163
Chapter 15	Parent/child friendships	181
Chapter 16	Framing	186
Chapter 17	What do you truly want for your child? (Professional sport vs active for life)	192
Chapter 18	Sport and the lessons of life	198

| Conclusion | 209 |
| Endnotes | 211 |

Part 1
How We Have Failed a Generation

Chapter 1
Every weekend in Australia

Being a parent is tough, let alone being a sporting parent. In many instances the upcoming Saturday weekly sporting fixture turns into a meticulous project to ensure that your child/children and their kit and equipment are packed, primed and delivered on time. When that mission is successfully completed, you have to do it all again the next weekend… and on it goes for another 4 months or so… and that's just one sporting season for one sport.

It can feel like an endless road trip across the State to a venue, especially if you get there and your child realises they've forgotten their boots or mouthguard. Arggggghhhh!

Every week in Australia approximately 3.2 million children (69%) participate in organised sport outside schooling hours.[1] That's a big market for everyone from school recruiters, private sporting academies, talent scouts and trainers. An estimated $2.3 billion is also spent yearly on children's sport and physical activity participation fees. The niche market that is youth sport has never been so strong.

And guess what? You're in it! Waist deep in it. Your pockets are heavily lined just to participate in it, before you even start thinking about it shaping your child's future.

Yet with all the latest technological resources and coaching opportunities at their fingertips (literally at the click of a button), as well as endless fields and facilities popping up from both your local council and privately funded organisations throughout the country, how have we got it so wrong with kids' sport?

Many of our kids are ill-equipped to even take part in weekly sporting fixtures, let alone at an elite level.[2,3]

Injury rates are through the roof! In fact, in New South Wales between 2005 and 2013, there were 20,034 hospitalisations for sports-related injuries for children aged between 5 and 15.[4] And over a 10-year period from 2005 to 2015 in Victoria alone, anterior cruciate ligament (ACL) injuries increased by 148%, with 98% occurring between the ages of 10 and 14![5]

When you and I were growing up, a knee reconstruction would have been a big deal. Dang! In fact for that to happen there would have to have been some serious s&*t go down! Or one hell of a car crash!

These days kids are missing season upon season for simply stepping 'unexpectedly' or having the inability to slow themselves down... but what about getting them to — wait for it, slow down and change direction at the same time?

I know, right. It's laughable at first, but it's simple things like this that have been lost to our youth of today. It leads to excessive hospital bills and plenty more gaming time while 'rehabilitating' (if you want to call it that, because you, I and anyone involved with kids knows that the likelihood of them completing rehabilitative exercises is non-existent on their own, especially trying to expect them to do them daily!).

Being a sporting parent, we can no longer refer to 'this generation' and all 'their' faults as a tokenistic opportunity to highlight their inadequacies while failing to acknowledge our responsibility for contributing to the problem. Not only have 'we' created them, but we have shaped the choices they make, the behaviours they display, and their need for the next latest and greatest 'thing' (whatever that may be) on the horizon.

Armed with the knowledge and tools in this book, you should be able to help your child to participate successfully in their chosen sporting endeavours, whatever sport/s that might be. Ideally, there'll be lots of them. But most importantly, you'll be able to help them to enjoy the opportunities and lessons that sport itself provides throughout their journey.

Lesson from the Field #1
Casey Dellacqua

Casey Dellacqua is a household name in Australia for tennis but she also has a diverse sporting background. Her successful professional tennis career spanned more than 16 years and saw her amass various titles in both singles and doubles. She also represented Australia at the 2008 Beijing Olympic games.

Casey achieved a career-high singles world ranking of 26, and 3 in doubles. She retired in 2018. She has a family of her own with partner Amanda and remains actively involved in tennis throughout Australia on a variety of levels. Casey shares invaluable insights into her journey as a professional athlete and now sporting parent.

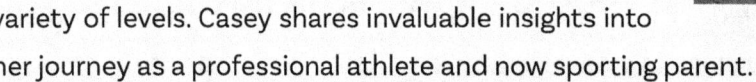

Growing up in Australia, how did you first get involved in sport?

I played just about every sport you could be offered as a kid growing up in Australia. Sport was inherent in me, growing up with my Dad having played AFL in the former WAFL competition and my Mum having played softball, tennis and netball.

I loved kicking the footy with my Dad!

As a kid, as far back as I can remember I was always being dragged around so my

Mum could continue to play sport. Weekends were pretty much spent following my parents to watch my Dad play footy.

My grandparents on my Mum's side even played tennis down at the local tennis club.

I really loved that aspect of being involved in a local sporting community.

My own participation in sport originally stemmed from those that my parents played. I played tennis, netball, T-ball, swimming, basketball... pretty much anything I could. It wasn't until I was about 13/14 years old that I stopped the majority of them and started to divert my attention towards tennis.

As I began to enjoy and take tennis more seriously, it was more the State coaches in WA at the time who encouraged me to go further. At that age it was important for me to not only play regularly but to compete with other girls my age.

Other girls were already travelling internationally, and I came to a crossroads. To progress further. I had to sacrifice other sports. With my coaches encouraging me, that's exactly what I did.

You're a household name for tennis in Australia. Growing up in a different generation to the modern athlete, do you see a distinct difference?

On the whole I feel like competitive sport has changed. Particularly with girls and their drop- out rates. There's been a big shift.

Speaking with a lot of my friends who have teenage girls, their interests are different. They prefer to go for walks or do certain types of physical activities that are different to competitive sport.

They're still leading an active lifestyle and making healthy choices, but it's very different to how I grew up and what I engaged in — competitive sport.

Growing up, all my friends regardless of their ability or sport played in competitions. They were active members of their local sporting club.

It almost seems like there is a real distinct divide between performance and participation in sport these days.

With tennis, a lot of players and parents feel like they need to specialise young. Because of that we fail to establish an effective pathway that encourages teenagers to remain engaged in sport for longer.

They may drop off and go to their local gym and do group fitness classes instead of staying in a sport.

Because it's very realistic for girls to now follow their dreams and accomplish success in sport, they tend to only see it one way. That you can either make it and succeed in a sport or be left with a grey area in the middle. This grey area leaves individuals dropping out if they're not competitive at a high level. They give up playing their sport.

To me that's a big loss because there's so many opportunities that are by-products of just participating in sport, without competing at a professional level.

I feel there's even a difference from State to State with tennis now in Australia. If we can embrace young athletes of today participating and being a part of their local tennis club community, they may eventually take the professional path.

Tennis centres in certain States are run very much like businesses. There is little sense of a collective community connection in them.

If we shift towards that community environment, you tend to grow a passion and love for the sport. A lifelong passion that encourages you to participate, regardless of the level.

So many of my friends I grew up with like Alicia Molik and others who have achieved great things in tennis still play today at their local club.

It's just different today though... You see so many parents just drop their kids off to play tennis and there's no parental involvement, even from a volunteer perspective. I remember growing up with my grandparents working in the canteen. These things still happen today, but more so in the regional areas and less and less in metro areas/capital cities.

The difference in team sports is they rely on volunteers for their sport to survive and prosper. But in a largely individual sport like tennis, parents aren't heavily involved at that grassroot participation level. It's coach driven instead with a business model to support it.

What works best is establishing connections and communities that encourage young players to play and remain in the sport for the love of it!

What do you see as the biggest challenges for the modern athlete?

- **Technology/social media**

There's no doubt about its impact, having started my career where you had to take a phone card overseas to remain in contact with your parents to where we're at now. Social media and other media put extra pressure on the athlete. It's hard enough being an athlete dealing with the pressures you place on yourself, let alone extrinsic life pressures being accentuated through the use of technology.

- **A balanced lifestyle**

Being an athlete and dealing with all the other relationships you have outside of sport is particularly important in setting yourself up for life after sport. Athletes need to make sure they're setting themselves up outside of sport.

This requires balance and mixing in circles from all walks of life. I believe the better balance you can have not only in your work but also in your relationships will inevitably set you up for success down the track.

You can have it all! From being a really top level player to being a good person simply by being kind and having a good work/life balance.

But it can be hard for the modern athlete with all of life's expectations.

- **Early specialisation**

These days I feel the expectation that 'if you don't specialise early you're not going to make it' is dangerous.
There's no doubt about it, there comes a time where you need to go all in… but it doesn't mean you specialise at all costs from the beginning.

I try to look at things with my own kids and what I would let them do. When I was 13 years old I won a trip to an academy in America through the Hopman Cup. My parents took me to the airport and put me on a plane. Would I be able to do that with my own kids — I don't know. At 16, I went to the Australian Institute of Sport and lived my dream of wanting to be a tennis player.

With your playing experience and time on tour, have you got any specific advice for sporting parents irrespective of the stage they're at on their journey?

I always had unconditional love and support from my parents from the very first day I picked up a racquet.

If I could give one bit of advice to parents it would be exactly that. Continually provide that unconditional love and support throughout their journey.

I was also fortunate to have parents that played high-level sport. I'm really grateful they pushed me to a point where I got the best out of myself. They knew how to challenge me as an individual with my personality traits to build qualities that enabled me to succeed.

There's a definite need for parents to talk to their kids about their sport. But I never felt my Mum or Dad were ever putting me down. I felt they were always supportive and encouraging regardless of where I ended up with my tennis.

For example, when I was 14 years old my Dad went and bought the beep test on cassette. It wasn't to pressure me into doing anything I didn't want to do. But simply to provide an opportunity where I would challenge myself.

With that love, support, and guidance they were able to get the best out of me — but it was never demanded.

You're a parent to three amazing kids (Blake, Andie and Jesse). Will there be any specific approach to how you view sport in their lives? And will there be any differences in how you approach Blake and Jesse vs Andie?

I've always been passionate about women in sport and the ability to have equal opportunities. Having a daughter it just becomes more apparent and clear that I want her to have the same opportunities. As we've evolved as a society over the years there won't be (and shouldn't be) any difference how I approach sport with all my kids.

My eldest is interested in everything. He loves sport and wants to play anything he can. We're happy to provide as much opportunity for him to explore everything. At his age, there's no need or rush to push him towards any sport in particular.

The sports we suggest he play are very much those we played when we were young. The flipside of that for me is that I wouldn't have thought much about football (soccer). But his mates at school play and he loves it! We support any of his suggestions and are open to him guiding us on what he wants to have a go at.

He's playing tennis and the fun part of it are the simple things. Just playing out the front of our place on the street or taking him down to the local park.

Amanda and I want him to play as many sports as possible. It's just good for kids overall body awareness!
Andie is already doing gymnastics and she's only 4! She was keen to do it so we enrolled her. I'd love her to try numerous other sports too, including some form of team sport.

Our journey as sporting parents has been fun. We're still learning and exploring things along the way.

It's interesting because our eldest (Blake) has only just stopped gymnastics. It's the one sport he didn't do with any of his mates. I think it just got to the point on Mondays that he began not wanting to go to gymnastics anymore. It was more that his mates weren't doing it too.

Blake's also displayed some great running ability so we just shifted and transferred the time he would have spent in gymnastics over to athletics.

Friendships also certainly play a big part in what sports kids are drawn to. While I've largely come from an individual sport, I loved doubles and other opportunities in my career like Fed Cup to play in a team because I just thrived! I enjoyed my sport more when I could celebrate victories with my team or others directly involved.

Fulfilment for me came from the traits and life skills that you learn when you're playing in a team. You're always playing for something more than yourself. I think that's a really important thing that's transferable to life!

At the end of the day, what will you define as success for your kids' participation in sport?

As a sporting parent I would define success as them choosing a sport they love competing in and for them to stay in that sport over their lifetime.

Sport is a vehicle for so many invaluable life lessons and contributions to communities around the world.

To find a sport you're passionate about that makes you want to stay involved irrespective of your accomplishments along the way… that to me is the true definition of success!

Chapter 2
Work, life, balance

If you're like me, you'll remember back to how hard your parents or parent worked to provide you with every opportunity to just participate in sport... let alone succeed at it.

The ironic thing is it's taken me all this time to realise how many sacrifices my parents made. Believe me, my participation didn't come easy. My Mum was a strong woman trying to juggle a business (3 retail shops) as well as my 3 other siblings and their sporting/social commitments.

My Dad was also a hard worker managing another business. Looking back, my Mum and Dad did an outstanding job in keeping us kids involved in so much sport and off the streets.

They separated in my early twenties. I can only imagine how tough these commitments are for single parents, especially those with multiple kids — #respect!

Nothing was ever a given in our household. The latest shoe release, sportswear item or piece of equipment (whether a tennis racquet, golf club, skateboard or BMX) would only be a one-off birthday or Christmas present. If something materialised outside of those days, it was pure magic!

Aussies are privileged to know, understand and respect hard work. These traits are also an essential prerequisite for a sporting parent. As I highlighted earlier, kids' sport isn't cheap and it's big business. So, what do those facts mean to you and the society we live in?

They mean big hours, long weeks and less time off (which actually translates to limited family time, in case you hadn't realised it). In some instances, both parents are also pursuing careers, promotions and overall life goals.

In many instances this is exactly what provides opportunity for our kids. But let's be honest here — more time working means less with your kids! This can't be replaced by simply booking them into your local 'elite' academy because you think it's not only the best for them, but because you try to justify to yourself that 'it's exactly what they need!'

Bu-bummm.... Epic fail!

As a sporting parent, I'm sure the thought has entered your head... more than once... that organised sport is the way to go. How good is it?! You can drop your kids off, pick them up, and in many instances even schedule your work or family errands around it. What's wrong with that? It's a win/win right?!

Unfortunately, sporting life just doesn't work that way. I'll even go a step further and say that this sentiment is one of the key reasons we are failing a generation. Organised sport has become such a hot commodity that our kids have forgotten to play. And by 'play', I'm referring to unstructured play. I'll talk more about unstructured play in chapters 6, 12 and 14 of this book.

Sporting life is about exploring learning. Failing, overcoming and understanding the process. As a sporting parent, you need to explore learning too! Your participation throughout this journey (and by 'participation' I'm referring to your active engagement, not scheduling coaches, academies, off-seasons, pre-seasons or anything that resembles what the pros do because little Johnny might be the next big thing — so is little Sally next door too). Stop kidding yourself!

Think Box

- Does your child participate in supplementary organised sport? (For example, squads, academies, private coaching, strength and conditioning sessions).   Yes / No

- Does your child only participate in scheduled sporting activities?
Yes / No

- In one week, how many times would your child participate in unstructured/free play? (for example, going to your local park/courts with a friend or friends).
    - 0
    - 1-2
    - 3-4

- Most importantly, how many times in the last month have you participated in any form of play/sport with your child? (For example, kicking a footy at the park).
    - 1-3
    - 4-5
    - >5

Balance is crucial to your child's success, not only in sport but in life.

Scheduled sport provides structure to your child's week. Kids crave structure. But if structure is all that exists, what happens when they get bored? We've created a generation that fails to keep themselves amused!

Encouraging your child to get outside and play at the park inspires creativity and learning. It can encourage a better understanding of specific sports through modifications in rules and environmental dimensions, as well as self-regulated social cohesion with other kids.

Remember when a simple game of force 'em back[6] turned into tackle footy in the street? I'm pretty certain there weren't sufficient numbers to make a legal team when I played in my neighbourhood, or that the street dimensions didn't translate exactly to our weekend sporting fixture. But we played anyway.

The best athletes in the world haven't got there through pre-programmed movement patterns, countless repetition or single sport participation as youths. Instead, they have learnt through fun, exploring different equipment, and via varying environmental constraints (in other words, they have taken a multi-sport approach). This approach drove them to better understand and eventually become obsessed to find the answer or to perfect a certain skill/technique/part of their game as they got older. I'll talk more about the multi-sport approach in chapter 7.

The irony is while you as an adult might be seeking your child's glossy finish and perfected skill by pursuing a jam-packed schedule for them, this is exactly what is limiting their freedom. The freedom to explore, learn and acquire along the way!

Don't get me wrong, structure certainly has its place, but you also need to provide a balance for both your child and yourself. Balance your own weekly schedule as well as your child's to ensure you can be an active participant on their journey.

If you answered a) to questions 3 and 4 in the *Think Box*, maybe it's time to find that balance...

Chapter 3
Technology

Let's be honest. If you're like me, the time it takes you to create a GIF (ask your son/daughter) could probably be better spent elsewhere.

What about trying to figure out how to add a story to your Instagram for the first time!

Or Tik Tok?! Hahaha seriously??? (Facepalm)

But that's not what this is about.

If you have ever found yourself yelling... Umm... I mean telling your child to 'put the iPad down!' or 'Get your face outta the screen!', you've probably realised it's a dead-end argument.

Perhaps you're a new (or soon-to-be) parent frowning upon others at your local cafe. The 'I'm never going to let my child spend that much time on their device!' brigade... only to realise at the first sign of trouble that 'it's just easier' or 'it's the only way we can get some peace and quiet!'.

... whichever side of the fence you find yourself on, you're losing an uphill battle.

It's not that kids are choosing to glue their faces to screens. Technology and society as a whole (from the educational system through to social interactions) shape it that way. This dependence on technology is having an effect on kids' 'hardware' (brains) and it's affecting their *ability to move*.

Unfortunately, whether you like it or not, their daily lives are driven by the use of technology. It's not the other way around. Schools across the country are becoming increasingly dependent on technology. So much so that it's a rarity for their syllabus to function without it.

If you don't believe me, ponder this question — if there was a blackout today, how much work could I actually get done? We all work in different professions, but seriously, ask your child the same question about schoolwork. The reality is many teachers would have difficulty coming up with a lesson that doesn't use technology in some capacity.

For an excellent read on the effect technology is having on our youth of today, I suggest you read *Teen Brain* by David Gillespie.

There is one thing for certain — technology isn't going away any time soon. The time spent using it in our daily lives is only going to increase. This unfortunately results in less time for kids to play. Less time to explore new opportunities. Less time to adapt to new environments. Less time to understand rules. Less time to socialise with friends... while playing. Less time for sporting activities. Less time away from the screen. Period.

Our kids' ability to move is largely dependent on their opportunity to play. In fact, many of the inadequacies in our youth of today can be attributed to their reduced time/opportunity to play.

The physical cost of technology dependence

How we move in our development years comes down to our exposure to movement. Think running, jumping, hopping, kicking, catching, and throwing. Many professionals label these as 'fundamental movement skills' or 'physical literacy'.[7,8,9,10]

These skills are ingrained early in your child's athletic journey. Sure, there will be movement adaptations along the way, such as during puberty (more on that in chapter 12), but ingrained, early movement patterns are what's most important. Early exposure promotes movement efficiency (coordination) and therefore a better, faster and more adaptable individual.

Limited early exposure to movement on the other hand results in poor running mechanics or the inability to even jump, let alone hop. Throw a ball in there for extra confusion. As parents, we're often quick to point out they can't kick or throw very well. Really?!

Our doctors and hospitals throughout the country are becoming busier with injuries sustained as a result of poor physical literacy. Fingers crossed your child doesn't ever need an operation. Unfortunately, the chances of that happening are increasing.

Strength and our body's ability to adapt and overcome is a result of the stresses placed on it. Fundamental movement skills are what strengthens your child's bones, muscles, and tendons. It's not your child's ability to stack weight on a bench press!

Dads, you probably hit the bench press as a teenager trying to get the size of

Arnie. Just wait for it, your child will be coming at you full tilt sooner than you know it asking for one for Christmas!

Strength inadequacies not only limit your child's ability to accomplish efficient movement patterns, they also significantly increase their likelihood of injury.

Did I mention the importance of play?...

The mental/emotional cost of technology dependence

The physical cost of technology is one thing. But to ignore its mental/emotional cost in shaping our future generation would be a travesty.

The physical costs are large enough for you to want to make a change to your parenting. But pause and reflect on the enormous mental impact technology is having on the development of your child's character as well. How they view the world will likely stop you dead in your tracks!

Technology (and in many instances the design of it or associated apps) increasingly demands a child's attention. Their immediate success or accomplishments in using it can be addictive. The greater the success or fulfilment, the more they want to use it. Simple.

If you're like me, it only seems like yesterday when you would wait patiently for what felt like an eternity for the dial-up internet to connect. Oh, but wait! Then a family friend would call the home phone just to say g'day to Mum or Dad and it would 'ruin your life' when the internet dropped out. Your parents would think, 'what's the big issue?!'

Your idea of technological advancement back then probably meant having *snakes* (the game) on your phone... or perhaps the ability to change the colour of your phone case to 'scream' your independence!

The youth of today are viewing the world through a different lens. All at the click of a button! They can choose what delivered food to order, find an answer on Google, check the weather, find their way home, or perhaps test the social acceptance of an outfit, action or ...

Social engagements may still be present... online... but *real time* engagement is very different!

Our kids can spend up to 12 hours per weekday on screen time (includes TVs, computers, smartphones, tablets, and video consoles) and in excess of 6 hours per day on weekends! This translates to an average of 31 — 43 hours per week for kids aged between 6 and 18. And did you know that Australian adults spend on average up to 5 hours per day on screen time too?[11] Surprised?

As parents, we are often quick to complain that our kids' lack resilience. Or the ability to commit and see things through. Technology plays an important role in that. Without the immediate success that technology offers, why would anyone want to take the long road?

Delayed gratification is the precise ingredient that enables success for sporting participants. But technology has diminished (and in many cases eradicated) delayed gratification for the youth of today. As technology continues to evolve and your child's dependence on it increases, so too will their desire for instant gratification. The by-product of technological advancements is very likely to be your child's lack of grit and a desire to chase easy solutions and/or accomplishments.

Sport (and its valuable lessons learnt along the journey) is important to set your child up for success. Emotional intelligence is a by-product of sporting participation. Unfortunately, the lack of social connection as a result of increased screen time reduces the opportunity for kids to learn lessons through sport and playing with their friends. They are ingredients to set them up for success.

Think Box

- Are you able to confidently say how many hours per week your child spends on a device?

    Yes / No

    If you answered 'No' (or would like just one example), you can check their phones:

    * iPhone — Settings > Screen Time (this will provide a daily breakdown of usage).

    * Android — Settings > Digital Well-being and Parental Controls > Tap the presented duration/time (this will provide a daily breakdown of usage)

- Where does your child fit? (factoring in all devices combined)
    a) < 20 hours
    b) 21–25 hours
    c) 26–30 hours
    d) > 30 hours

Technology and its use is likely to hinder your child's physical and mental/emotional well-being. As a sporting parent, it's important to be aware of that and to have a plan in place to minimise its negative impact, because technology isn't going away anytime soon!

Chapter 4
Fundamental movement skills

Fundamental movement skills lay the foundation for your child's success and advancement along the way. As highlighted in chapter 3, they include running, jumping, hopping, kicking, catching, throwing, and even tumbling.

Like the alphabet in literacy, these skills are essential building blocks for children to progress in their athletic journey. But the youth of today aren't developing these skills early enough or often enough.

Think back to playing in the school playground. As a girl growing up it was the norm to play hopscotch. Remember? Take a walk throughout any suburban street in Australia and you would stumble across almost Van Gogh-like chalk renditions of your favourite game. Combined with your imagination, the options were endless.

Even as a young fella, you may not have spent your lunch times playing with girls in your primary school years — but you sure as hell would have at least run through one or two hopscotch games in your time to show them how it's done (or at least how you thought it was done at the time)!

Fellas — remember 'brandings'?! When you got your mate so good it marked or in the odd instance would drop him, only for it to be all forgotten about by the time the bell rang to end recess/lunch... ready to get the crew together again tomorrow. There was always that mate who had a great throw or arm!

Or in the mid-late 90s when political correctness started to introduce its putrid self (and the fun police started flashing their badges) and you were left playing 'throws' because branding was 'dangerous'. Standing at the end of the court/field and whoever could launch the tennis ball the furthest was the big dog in town?

But simply put, our youth of today (yes remember they're 'our' because we created them) aren't fit to play sport. Regardless of how much the 'elite' academy they might be enrolled in costs, our youth are fundamentally flawed. The sooner we accept that fact, the greater ownership we have of the problem and the faster we can rectify it.

Remember what I said earlier about the rising number of kids' sporting injuries? Below are just some examples of how we have created a population of *exposed* youth who are ready and waiting for your local sports physician's blade.

- Failing to provide the freedom of 'play'. From going to their local park with mates to outlawing games deemed 'unsafe' in the playground.
- Providing our kids with so much opportunity that anything outside of 'structured' play (lessons/organised sport) just simply isn't available to them.
- Overcommitting our child's weekly schedule, because we think we're providing them with the 'best opportunity' to succeed. More on this in chapters 6 and 13 in the book.
- Making them specialise in a particular sport early because we think that's the best way for them to succeed.
- Participating in one sport all year-round at the exclusion of others, because we think that any missed opportunity will leave little Johnny or Alisha behind the eight ball.
- Seeking private coaching to supplement our child's sport so they can participate in more 'sport-specific' training programs, whether that be strength and conditioning/performance-based or one-on-one, sport-specific coaching.

There is nothing intrinsically wrong with one-on-one coaching in individual, skills-based sports like tennis, but your child shouldn't be having these sessions several times per week. The same principle applies to physical preparation/fitness sessions for children.

Understandably, different sports have different training requirements. Certain sports or player positions within them may be more technical in nature. In this instance, one-on-one coaching may be warranted and normal. But you shouldn't be doing it as a 'norm' or trying to fill your child's week in order to get a step in front of their competition (other kids).

Your light bulbs might have just gone off, and you're acknowledging that you've done at least 1 (if not 2 or more) of these things. 'Guilty!', you say, raising your hand sheepishly.

Or you might be staring at this page, thinking 'bull-sh&*t!'. What does this bloke know anyway?!', while reciting examples of all the greatest who have made it in professional sport over the years having done this or that. Play on ….

Now for the fun part. I want you to try the following practical tests that are designed to not only show you what I'm talking about, but also to allow you to understand exactly how fundamental movement skills apply to your child. Are you up for the challenge?*

Disclaimer — because we live in the politically correct and increasingly litigious age, I have to remind you of the obvious. It's entirely your choice whether you want to do the following 4 standard tests with your child (or not), and entirely your responsibility to provide appropriate supervision.

Test #1 (Triple hop)

- Ask your child to hop 3 times (vertically on a mark) and land (with a 3-second hold between each hop) without falling over or putting their other foot on the ground to prevent them from stumbling.

Can they maintain balance in the absence of falling over **Yes / No**

Can they do so successfully on both legs: right and left leg? **Yes / No**

If your child can, prove it. Simply tag @thesportingparent #physicalchallenge for the chance to be mentioned!

Progression:
- ask your child to hop 3 times (horizontally for *distance*) and land (with a 3-second hold between each hop) without falling over or putting their other foot on the ground to prevent them from stumbling.

Can they maintain balance in the absence of falling over? **Yes / No**

Can they do so successfully on both legs: right and left leg? **Yes / No**

Test #2 (Standing broad jump)

- Ask your child to jump (horizontally for *distance*) and land (with a 3-second hold) without falling over or taking a step forward on the ground to prevent them from stumbling.

Chapter 4 Fundamental movement skills

Can they maintain balance in the absence of falling over? **Yes / No**

How far do they travel? (Measure from their toes at the start to their heel after they jump). See below for an age-based comparison.[12]

Standing Broad Jump- Age Based Norms

AGE	BOYS	GIRLS
9-11 yrs	135 cm	123 cm
12-15 yrs	167 cm	141 cm

Remember! @thesportingparent #physicalchallenge for the chance to be mentioned!

Test #3 (Plank shoulder tap)

Ask your child to:

- assume the push-up position (with arms straight and feet shoulder-width apart).
- take one hand off the ground and touch their opposite shoulder, holding that position for 3 seconds. They should then do the same for the opposite shoulder.
- continue alternating between shoulders until their hip alignment suffers.

Can they maintain hip alignment on both arms for 3 seconds? **Yes / No**

How many repetitions can they complete?

Have you @thesportingparent #physicalchallenge yet? If you didn't snap it, it didn't happen!

Test #4 (Forward roll)

Find a soft surface — ideally grass — and ask your child to:

- squat down and place their hands on the ground, with their weight evenly distributed between the balls of their feet and the palms of their hands.
- tuck their chin to their chest.
- shift their weight onto their hands, progressing to roll onto their upper back.
- grasp their shins using both hands during the roll to maintain their tight tuck.
- upon completing the roll, release their shin grasps.
- push through with both feet to finish in a tall, standing position.*

* **Tip** — The greater the transition of weight distribution from feet to hands prior to commencing the roll, the more momentum your child will have to complete the roll successfully by finishing in a standing position

Was your child able to complete this test? **Yes / No**

Did they complete it successfully the 1st time? **Yes / No**

Oooooh, we're going to see some epic fails here... with you as the sporting parent staring in stunned disbelief and a cheeky 'are you for real?!'

Hahaha, let's see it @thesportingparent #physicalchallenge.

Now having completed the tests (if not all, at least 1), you're either down with my 'vibe', or thinking your kid's killing it! Well guess what, they may be.

The purpose of the tests is to give you real-time examples of fundamental movement skills. There is no bigger real-time test than your own child. Even the most competitive sporting parent will acknowledge if their child is visibly struggling — it's that simple.

So well done for completing the tests, whichever end of the continuum your child fell on.

The reality is that kids today aren't exposed to what we were as youths. So how can we expect the same outcomes? Physical Education (PE) classes have become a legal minefield, transforming into Physical Development Health and Physical Education (PDHPE). This has meant more theory and less of the good (physical) stuff.

We've become so overprotective of our little bundle of joys that things like gymnastics have been taken out of the curriculum for being too hazardous. Or at the very least, the precise gymnastics' activities that made you and I sink or swim (and think seriously about whether we were going to commit to that somersault off the vault) are precisely what have been taken out.

Ask your child when was the last time they completed a tumble roll in PDHPE. The reality is they haven't, for fear of the school being sued.

The next time you watch your child take the court/field, run for a ball, produce an air swing or kick, ask yourself if they are adequately prepared to participate in sport. Do they have the necessary fundamental movement skills?

Chapter 5
Taking ownership

As parents, we all have an opinion on *this generation*. As sporting parents and armed with the knowledge you've accumulated so far reading this book, I'm sure you've thought twice about how to approach at least one thing differently.

How many times have you as a sporting parent said one of the following:

- 'This generation lacks resilience.'
- 'This generation is so spoilt.'
- 'This generation always has everything given to them.'
- 'That's the problem with this generation.'
- 'In my time, we used to...'

Wait for it... Give yourself an uppercut!
No, seriously — give yourself an uppercut because *we* have created this generation (not *them*)!

You're either thinking 'yeah, he's got a point' or 'this bloke's kidding himself!'.

OK, you don't believe me? Well let's flip the script with *your* actions now. How many times have you as a parent (note that I said 'parent', not 'sporting parent') done any of the following?

- Your kid gets dropped and you confront the coach.
- Your kid gets played out of position and you agree with your child — it's bullsh&*t!
- You're unhappy with an aspect of your child's participation in a particular season and as a result change teams or even schools.
- At least once you have screamed from the sideline, 'Referee?!'
- You have proudly boasted of your child's junior ranking or making the U/8, 10, or even 12's representative team.

Are you still standing from the previous uppercuts? If so — give yourself another one!

We have created this generation! The sooner we accept it, the faster we as sporting parents can lead through our actions and work towards a brighter future (more on that in Part 3).

As a parent you will have heard many times over that our kids mirror our actions. And let's be honest, we can't be perfect all the time. But can't we at least *try* to be our best?! Isn't that why you're reading this book? Because you want to do what you can to ensure your child succeeds not only in sport, but in life?

The only way this generation is likely to change is through our actions as sporting parents and the decisions we make for them. Over time, this will not only ensure we exhibit positive traits and shift the curve of this generation, it will also empower us as sporting parents to be positive role models for our children.

In the last chapter, you put your kid/s to the test. Now it's your turn. This weekend (or at your child's next sporting fixture), I want you to complete the following.

Think Box

Parental Test (White Line Fever Checklist)

Instructions

- Take a photo of the below checklist.

- Message it to another parent you usually watch your child's game with (but not your partner*).

- Ask the other parent to read it to familiarise themselves prior to kick off/gun fire/1st ball/1st point. Get your associate to mark how many instances their response to your behaviour is Y.

- Don't discuss the test at all during the fixture.

- Shout them a coffee/tea/or whatever rocks their boat for giving you the most important 5 minutes of your child's journey.

- Tag @thesportingparent #passedthetest to highlight your commitment.

*Note — I did say the test is to be completed by another parent who is not your partner. This is because many parents get so worked up watching they're kids play that they don't realise how they're behaving. It's often easier for your partner to ignore you rather than having to justify their 'white line fever' case to you in front of the kids on the car ride home.

Checklist

1. At any stage did I shout out to the referee or an official?   Yes / No

2. At any stage did I comment to anyone who would care to listen about a referee/umpire/official's decision or their capabilities?   Yes / No

3. Did I call out to my child's coach?   Yes / No

4. Did I instruct my child's coach about how to make a change/appeal a decision/make a substitute?   Yes / No

5. Did I contribute to the half-time address to the players?   Yes / No

6. Did I move along the sideline, fence or court with the position of play? In some instances finding myself separate from other parents).   Yes / No

7. Under any circumstance did I use profanities? Even if just to a mate/friend whose kids are on the same team?   Yes / No

8. Was the first thing I said to my child at the end of the game/match related to their performance?   Yes / No

Interpretation of results:

- If you score 1 Yes and 7 No's, don't lose too much sleep over it. It simply means you're a passionate parent.... Well unless it was you in the headlines confronting the referee in the carpark resulting in a life ban from attending your child's sporting events! #douche!

- If for any reason you thought twice about a particular action while watching your child compete, great! This means you're still functional during your child's sport and not white lining it!

We will go into greater detail in chapter 14 on many issues related to white line fever, but the *Think Box* checklist is a brilliant litmus test.

If you never do any self-reflection, how can you ever improve as a sporting parent? How you fared isn't going to shape your child's future. But what you do from here on and how you absorb the information presented in the remainder of this book will shape it though.

It will also shape how your child views you in their world. What impact are you going to make on your child's life throughout their sporting journey?

Part 2
Building the Foundations

Chapter 6
Specialisation

For those new to the world of kids' sport or those with their head in the sand, the concept of sport specialisation is more than a decade-old debate.

It's nothing new... but frequently ignored or overlooked.

Google the term 'sport specialisation' and there's a mass of articles, videos and literature available. If you ever want to go down a rabbit hole, this is the topic to search!

But what does sport specialisation really mean for you and your child? Arm yourself with the information in this chapter to empower yourself to set your child up to succeed.

Simply put, *sport specialisation* is the intense focus on a particular sport at the exclusion of others. With an adult mindset, it only seems logical that your child should do that to succeed in a particular sport. Right?

Enter the **CEO parent**. CEO parents are those that attack their kids' sporting endeavours with the business acumen of a well-versed business plan or financial forecast. Projected targets or KPIs are established with various rep teams and opportunities identified.

According to CEO parents, specialising in one sport is the only way. They also often believe specialised coaching is the only way for their child to achieve their 'true potential'.
Any detour exploring other sports is only wasting time and reducing the likelihood of their child's success.

But here's the thing. Those beliefs couldn't be further from the truth! It's only as adults and through our own experience that some parents believe honing in on a particular sport and eliminating all other *peripheral noise* (being other sports) will fast-track their child and ensure success.

Kids fail to learn many lessons through sport specialisation. The absence of unstructured play and the freedom to explore is substituted for strict, structured play that often includes excessive private lessons, academies, squads, and strength and conditioning sessions.

Seasonal variation is a great way to avoid sport specialisation. The beauty of summer versus winter sports is the ability to 'put one down' so to speak and pick it back up 'next season'. Kids generally require a different skill set from one sport to the next, enhancing their fundamental movement skills.

Substituting a running, or swimming-based sport for racquet, bat or ball sport are all exceptional ways to target various physical qualities in your child's journey. You may even substitute one ball sport for another (e.g. basketball/netball for AFL/football).

How many times have you heard about a national sporting hero also being good at another sport? Think Ash Barty from tennis to cricket and back. Michael Jordan and baseball. Upcoming juniors as well. Some may come to a crossroad of having to choose between sports in order to pursue one at the highest level.

Another big factor to consider in early sport specialisation is injury rates. We'll go into this in greater detail later in Part 2, but many bookings for sports physicians are for kids' injuries associated with overuse. This overuse is a result of not only a weekly schedule with enough sessions packed in to put professional sport to shame, but also from completing 'sport-specific training'. So much training that the child's progress is sabotaged by having to spend time out of the sport in the rehabilitation zone.

I once observed a school sport setting where the weekly rugby development program schedule outshone the Wallabies' weekly training commitments!

Throw schooling and the normal adolescent daily challenges into the mix and it was a recipe for disaster. It didn't take long for the program to 'give itself an uppercut' and morph into an updated program of 'realism'.

Overuse injuries are common during adolescent growth periods. If you stumble across them, don't sweat it. But if they are encouraged by your decisions as a CEO parent, you'll most certainly set yourself up for voluntary administration!

Now, before you start arcing up because your child is in a sport that has year-round participation like swimming, gymnastics or tennis, I want you to consider the following:

- it's OK to participate in both year-round sports and seasonal sports.
- limit your child's intensity/commitment to year-round sports.
- don't overcommit by choosing to participate in another sport. Instead, limit the exposure to each sport or the pendulum swinging too far in either direction.
- sport participation is one thing, supplementary training is another. Once again, don't over commit!
- if not participating year-round means missing selection in a squad or academy in the early days (<12 years), so be it. The long game will ensure future success, not youth-level success.

Another way to approach this sport specialisation challenge is to encourage your child to do another sport that uses some of the same skills they have but that also requires them to develop others. For example:

- swimming for nippers
- football for futsal
- field-based sports for athletics/cross-country.

Think Box

- Does your child participate in one particular sport all year-round?   Yes / No

- Has your child ever participated in a sport at the exclusion of others?   Yes / No

- Have you ever tried to get your child out of a sporting commitment in favour of another?   Yes / No

- Has your child participated in sport-specific activities to better themselves over an 'off-season'?   Yes / No

Remember, a successful sporting journey is about exploring other sports, not necessarily eradicating or completely sacrificing one sport at the cost of another.

The older your child gets, the more direct and intense focus can be placed on a particular sport. When, you ask? As a general rule of thumb, around 16 years of age and beyond. However, it might be slightly earlier in some sports.

Istyvan Balyi, who was a pioneer in the long-term athletic development (LTAD) space, categorised this as the 'training to compete' stage. Facets of sport participation and associated training can be targeted towards a competition calendar/season. This enables the athlete to physiologically adapt and to increase their sport-specific learning and understanding before transitioning into the next phase, 'training to win'.[13]

Looking at your child's sporting journey as the pyramid of commitment illustrated below is a great guide.

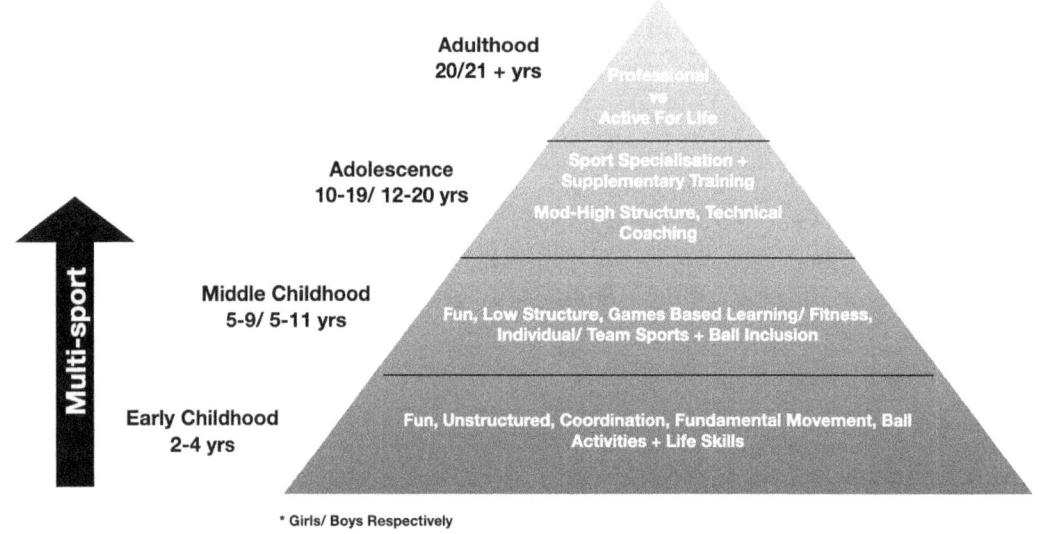

Image 1. Sport sampling pyramid

The bottom line when it comes to your child's participation in sport is to encourage them to sample other sports and to sample them frequently. The foundational years are what will set your child up for success down the track. Remember, it's about playing the long game as a sporting parent. We can't complain about this generation if we're not prepared to embrace the long-haul ourselves.

Chapter 6 Specialisation

Lesson from the Field #2
Tim Walsh

Tim Walsh is the Head Coach of the Aussie Men's Sevens team at Rugby Australia. He is also a former professional rugby player, having played Super Rugby for the QLD Reds, internationally throughout Europe and captaining the Aussie Men's Sevens himself prior to commencing his coaching career.

Tim is the epitome of the modern coach. He's human in his approach, resourceful and adaptable. Successful in transitioning from player to coach and drawing on his playing

experience, he continues to progress through the modern era. His coaching credentials were cemented when he guided the Aussie Women's Sevens team to a gold medal at the 2016 Rio Olympics.

Did you play various sports as a child growing up in Australia?

Absolutely! I lived for sport as a kid. Any kind and believe me, I tried everything.

My favourite subjects at school were recess, PE and lunchtime. Any spare minute would be taken up trying to dislocate my wrist bowling a wrong'un, kicking a footy left foot through a tree, or trying to trounce my old man for the first time at ping pong.

If you asked me as a kid I confidently would have said I would be playing for the Wallabies in winter and the Australian cricket team in the summer.

The sports I participated in growing up included:

- tennis
- Little Athletics
- AFL
- rugby
- cricket
- cross country
- swimming
- table tennis
- ++++

Transitioning into your career as a coach, have you felt the need for the early specialisation of kids in sport nowadays?

Put simply, no! Is there room for some kind of balance? Definitely.

The beauty of playing a multitude of different sports is it enables you to discover your true passion. It also enhances your ability to execute skills and make better decisions. I don't see a difference from when I was growing up. Diverse experiences and skill acquisition go hand in hand making you a better athlete and a more balanced person.

Specialising only really becomes relevant later in life when you have developed a passion for a particular sport. You may have decided you want to have a real crack and play in the best teams or to compete against the best players. Specialisation then improves your overall performance.

You've had the pleasure of working with some impressive athletes as a coach. Have you come across many athletes who have been successful in more than one sport? Or who perhaps transitioned into another sport after you coached them?

My time with the Aussie Women's Sevens team was essentially a blank canvas. It was an enabler to select and then recruit the best athletes from non-traditional rugby backgrounds.

Throughout my playing and coaching career I've always found that the best athletes have played just about everything. They happened to be pretty good at their majority of sports too.

I truly believe the exposure and experience of playing other sports gave them a competitive advantage. It enabled them to view their eventual chosen sport differently (from a cognitive perspective), acquire/contribute different skills (technically) and move efficiently (physically).

Irrespective of their tools used — a tennis racquet, bowling ball, golf club or a basketball, they more than likely had played a sport before and excelled at it. If they hadn't, they picked it up very quickly.

I've had the privilege to coach many Rugby Sevens' athletes who had represented Australia in their previous sporting careers. I've also had several transitions into other elite level sports after their Rugby Sevens' careers, such as into the WAFL and NRLW to name a couple.

In my mind, you epitomise the modern coach. You're adaptive, explorative and resourceful in your coaching methods. Have you drawn (or do you draw) coaching methods from other sports? And if so, do you see a 'transfer' from certain drills that could be applied across a variety of sports?

Most definitely. I personally have had many experiences immersing myself in other sports and learning from them. I've not only adapted skill-based drills to our sport, but I've investigated other coaches — how they communicate, measure, review or analyse performances. What systems, procedures and structures they use to operate.

There are so many creative and talented organisations that have the ability to teach you an abundance of lessons if you're prepared to open yourself up and explore the opportunities.

The obvious ones that come straight to mind for Rugby Sevens revolve around restart possession. We have learnt invaluable insights from AFL. Specifically around technique and positioning in order to win the aerial battle translates to our game.

Another example would be the mental preparation for a consistent golf swing. That's very relevant to the mental rehearsal for our restart kicking.

Nothing is off-limits. If you're not seeking new ideas or ways to improve outside your regular domain, you're not evolving as a coach!

I hear you stepped it up a notch taking advantage of the COVID-19-enforced downtime to coach your son's U/6 rugby side?

Despite being the longest hours of my week and the most challenging, it was without a doubt rewarding. I encourage all parents to give it a crack!

My advice to parents would be to expose and encourage your kids to dabble in a variety of sports. Mine do and will continue to throughout their sporting journey.

Eventually kids gravitate to the sport they enjoy the most and are genuinely passionate about. That results in a more engaged and focused athlete. It also nurtures a more open attitude to skill acquisition and problem solving.

How would you define success for your own kids' participation in sport?

Competitive sport provides physical, social and psychological benefits not only to individuals, but to communities as a whole. Sport transcends cultures and speaks a universal language.

As a sporting parent, success for my kids is for them to benefit from all that sport has to offer. To learn and grow as individuals within the environment of sport. To list them all would take up pages of this book!

I'd love for all the sporting parents out there to each take a moment and list a couple of physical, social and psychological benefits that sport provides to them as an individual, and more importantly, to their family.

Chapter 7
Sport selection

Sport selection for your child more often than not runs deep. So deep it may have been the sport you played as a kid. Your father, and even maybe your father's father.

There's a strong emotional attachment to it.

For me, I came from a big 'tennis family'. Several of my aunties/uncles on my Mum's side were involved in coaching and running their own tennis complexes/facilities. Even on my Dad's side, my cousins had a tennis court growing up.

So there's no prize for guessing the first sport I picked up and naturally became accustomed to!

There was many a Christmas showdown, whether it was with my cousins or an all-in with multiple courts occupied by aunties, uncles, parents, cousins and the like (ah, the memories!).

Chapter 7 Sport selection

My closest sibling (age-wise) was my older brother. He dabbled in tennis but then found a passion for golf. How did that happen you might ask? Well my Dad played golf, as did his father. My grandfather even had an international manufacturing business that produced golf bags/products.

Even now, having become a father myself and a 'certified' sporting parent (haha, well sort of), will my son be walking onto a tennis court? Absolutely... in due course ☺

So yep... sport selection runs deep.

No doubt you're nodding your head in agreement! Why wouldn't you? Your childhood sport probably brings you such fond memories and a sense of nostalgia, even more so now when you see your son/daughter donning your local team kit (or in my case, picking up my tennis racquet of choice).

If this wasn't you, maybe you became an obsessed, armchair sports fan following a particular sport. Whether your choice was netball, rugby, football or whatever, you were obsessed. You never played it, but your garage is littered with your favourite team colours.

So, which sport are you recommending to your child?... You got it!

Then there are the other types of parents. You know the ones, they're obsessed, relentless and impulsive. Heck, they might even kick up a sh*#tstorm over some overpriced fish in the player lounge out the back at the Australian Open (jokes). No seriously, they see their child as their meal ticket out of wherever they are in life. They are so passionate they become enraged and eventually (you guessed it), their kids don't talk to them much later in life.

Chapter 7 Sport selection

But that's other parents — not you! So we don't need to spend much time on the issue. But we all know one. It just wouldn't be Australia (or sport) without one!

Getting back to sport selection, what if there's greater opportunity for your child through being exposed to other sports? Or even sports that might enhance your child's ability in your sport of choice?

In Part 1, we delved into the issue that the youth of today simply aren't physically well equipped for the demands of sport. Completing the physical tests in chapter 4 with your child may well have cemented this view for you.

Then there is the challenge of maturation as an extra hurdle for your child to stumble through.

Here's the thing — not only is navigating your way through kids' sport confusing enough, try finding a sport that continues to keep them happy, challenged and with a positive peer group…

One of the most common questions I get asked is, 'What's the best sport for my child to play?'

Now, it would be easy for me to fall back into that *emotional connection* I highlighted earlier and simply choose sports I'm interested in. Like tennis… But no! The sports I suggest are ones to compensate for modern kids' lack of physical adequacy that also have beneficial by-products of participation.

In other words, sports you may never have thought of that will enhance your child's physical development through participation — win:win.

To enhance your understanding throughout the stages of your little cherub's maturation/development I've even categorised them based on Oliver and Lloyd's Youth Physical Development Model (which I'll talk further about in chapter 12).

Early childhood (ages 2–4)

Gymnastics

While you may have dabbled in gymnastics as a youth in the dreaded PE class, the difference these days is that it used to be a mandatory component. Unfortunately, for a variety of reasons (I'll give you one — legal repercussions), the youth of today simply aren't exposed to it.

That's right, you may not have been aware but in the majority of instances gymnastics is simply non-existent in today's syllabus. At least not to the extent it used to be, if at all. If you don't believe me or are shocked to read this, go and ask your child now! If they do any gymnastics, it's most likely an outsourced program. Even then, their limited exposure to it prevents many of the activities that encouraged you to sink or swim as a youth. Forward rolls, somersaults, round offs, etc. are generally a 'no-go' zone.

'Wow!,' you might think. And we wonder why our youth of today look awkward the first time they get on a trampoline. You know the ones that are all enclosed, looking like an octagon out of an MMA bout. Because legally no company these days will dare venture into the abyss of a child getting jammed in the springs or simply bouncing off onto the ground.

Back in the day, you may have issued a dare to a kid in your neighbourhood to do a somersault off one of those trampolines and to land on the ground! (Yep — whack!).

The answer is simple. Enrol your child in gymnastics early because the benefits are endless. They encourage your child to increase what us geeks call their 'kinaesthetic awareness'. Translated simply, it increases their body's ability to 'feel itself' in its surrounding environment... Coordination!

Swimming

Simply put, this is a life skill! I've met far too many kids who can't swim. Adults for that matter too — yep, absolutely. Professional athletes who can't even go to the beach as part of their recovery processes because they simply can't swim. I know, right?! We live in Australia, renowned for our sunny beaches and backyard pool parties. Yet so often this fundamental skill is overlooked along some parenting journeys.

Lessons are expensive, time is limited, and you can only do it in summer. Whatever excuses some parents tell themselves, they quite simply just don't stack up against their other specialised coaching, structured practice or jam-packed weekly training schedules.

In a matter of life and death, I'm guessing 100% of you would choose to enrol your kids if you had a crystal ball. Well unfortunately you don't, so play it safe and make sure your child learns how to swim...early!

By the way, swimming is excellent for optimising your child's aerobic capacity. For those asthmatic kids swarming our school enrolments, this is a no brainer! A life skill with the benefits of enhanced physical fitness.

Middle childhood (ages 5-9 for girls, 5-11 for boys)

Athletics

As you may have discovered when doing the tests in chapter 4 with your child, our youth struggle with what we assume is the norm of playing based on our growing up journey. Simple tasks like running and jumping often don't appear that simple after all. Disguised by specialist coaching, footwork patterns and the technicalities of sport-specific movements in isolation, these simple tasks often prove the physical literacy inadequacies of today's youth.

Yet some parents are happy to seek the services of a specialised sprint coach for their child?!

If you've already developed their kinaesthetic awareness in early childhood via gymnastics and swimming, it's only logical to build on their athletic prowess. By that I mean enrol them in Little Athletics. They will participate in multiple activities that not only continue to build on their kinaesthetic awareness, it will translate it into the athletic space. Running, jumping, landing and throwing, all in the name of fun while building relationships with their peers in the process.

That speed you're seeking later in your child's sporting endeavours often comes not from an increase in strength/power but from enhanced mechanics increasing their efficiency. So why not invest early as part of the journey, that way it will free up time and money down the track that can be better invested elsewhere!

Brazilian Jiu-Jitsu

I know what you're probably thinking — my son/daughter isn't participating in 'fighting' or anything of the sort! OK, firstly let me start by saying I understand what you're referring to. But simply put, I tend to disagree. Here's why.

With the general physical inadequacy in today's youth, Brazilian Jiu-Jitsu is not only relevant to their fundamental movement skills but also to their strength development. While it may not be appropriate to throw your daughter under a bar trying to squat the house down or for her bench press numbers to be up there with her Dad and his mates in the shed, it's in your child's best interests to increase their strength. Part of this equation is to do with injuries — their likelihood of occurring and preventing them.

While specialised coaching is often sought by certain parents in the development space, it isn't the be-all and end-all. While strength is very important for children progressing through their athletic journey, it should complement their athleticism rather than it being done in isolation. Especially this early in the journey!

Their athletic ability is built upon and translated into actions more likely to aid their sporting endeavours, so we can't forget about that kinaesthetic awareness. Brazilian Jiu-Jitsu encourages them to build upon their individual gymnastics moves against external resistance (the environment/a partner). They will be challenged to lift, pull, push and turn their opponent while rolling, landing and falling themselves. The sought-after strength will be a by-product of their movement and their understanding of their environment.

Tennis

OK, while it's easy for me to suggest tennis due to my own childhood background, I'm simply suggesting an individual rather than a team ball sport. Here's why.

Hand-eye coordination is an important skill in child development, particularly prior to that adolescent growth spurt (peak height velocity — PHV). PHV refers to the greatest amount of growth over the shortest period of time as kids mature. Kinaesthetically they will be in a far better position if they are confident in their hand-eye coordination as they enter this adolescent stage.

Tennis is a great way to encourage kids' multi-directional, agile movement in conjunction with utilising their upper body with a self-directed, results-based outcome. In other words, they will know if the ball has gone in the court, been captured by the net or blocked by the back fence!

Combining athletic movements (running, decelerating and changing direction) with an environmentally restricted scenario (a tennis court) encourages kids to independently self-regulate their actions.

Adolescence stage #1 (ages 10-14 for girls, 12-15 for boys)

Football codes

Hand-eye/eye-foot coordination is the main objective here. Throw in contact, (yes even in football or as we say in Australia, 'soccer', said in my Aussiest bogan accent), cardiovascular fitness and teamwork… This is a win-win!

Your child is going to go through a rapid growth spurt during this stage. This is where all the previously planned sporting experimentation will assist in limiting the 'Bambi-like phenomenon'. Even gangly kids with the right sporting journey can effectively manage to put one foot in-front of the other during this growth phase. And perhaps even kick a ball, tackle a player or pass well in the process.

With a decent cardiovascular system developed from having already engaged in the right childhood activities, your adolescent will progressively adapt physiologically and their heart rate will begin to shine. In due course...

Team-based sports during adolescence are crucial for developing social cohesion with their peers. While little Johnny/Sophia may well begin to object to everything you as a parent request of them during this adolescent stage (plus more), participating in team activities will encourage them without us 'grown adults' telling them that life 'isn't just on their terms!'

Friendships are made. Heated exchanges may also occur on the odd occasion due to their adolescent fire. But they will help to not only shape your child's character but to set them up for future relationships in life!

Basketball/Netball

These are team-based hand-eye coordination sports that can help you take a multi-sport approach over various seasons.

Cross-Country

Team-based sports are one thing, but maintaining that individual edge is another. Your child needs to understand the importance of independence and self-belief. They need to be encouraged to be accountable for their own success. Cross-country running is great for that. Their enhanced cardiovascular fitness during adolescence will also coincide with the adaptations going on in their heart.

Adolescence stage #2 (ages 15-19 for girls, 16-20 for boys)

This is the stage of independence and autonomy, while you still will put a cap on their social engagements to an extent. You don't want them to be out until all hours of the morning partying.

Adolescents in this stage explore friendship circles as they dabble with the concept of social acceptance. The freedom to choose is thrust upon them. This is not only empowering for their development, but also a step in the journey towards adulthood.

This independent time is often where their enjoyment for a particular sport fuels their passion. This passion intensifies their desire to succeed, and as a result, their self-driven autonomy. Their training, exploration and the intensity of competition rises. Unlike the early maturation stage, sports at this stage will cement the level of engagement your child has.

The multi-sport approach can still be encouraged. However, with the increase in competition, more opportunity to prepare and potential rep/institute/team selection, a year-round participation is likely to start occurring during this phase.

So, what sport you might ask? Well, that's up to your adolescent. Notice I said 'your adolescent' — not you. 😉

Playing professional sport or simply remaining active for life are two sides of the spectrum that may define what success means to you as a sporting parent. There is no right or wrong in that regard. Remember, this is your journey as a sporting parent and your definition of success — no one else's.

Chapter 7   Sport selection

Adulthood (ages 20+ for girls, 21+ for boys)

Limitless...

As a sporting parent, your job is done. You've provided opportunities, contributed to shaping your child's character, instilled values, and empowered them with the ability to be independent and to choose what they enjoy.

... Notice that I did say 'enjoy'.

If you have reached this stage and your child (now adult) still enjoys playing sport, I applaud you as a sporting parent for your hard work and years of dedication. Your child/adult will have quality peer groups developed through sport. Engaging in physical activity irrespective of the level they eventually reached is the norm for them, along with making healthier lifestyle choices.

Now that's winning right there! 😊 (insert warm and fuzzy feeling here — because you deserve it!).

Who knows, your legacy as a sporting parent may continue when your kids have kids of their own…

Think Box

1. What stage is your child at in their stage of development? (Circle appropriate answer).

- Early Childhood

- Middle Childhood

- Adolescence Stage #1

- Adolescence Stage #2

- Adulthood

2. Are you helping them to develop appropriate physical traits for their stage of development with your sport selection? (Circle appropriate answer).

   a. Yes
   b. No

3. If you answered 'No' to question 2, how could you improve their future sporting selection?

4. If you circled c-e) in question 1, did your child's sporting participation resemble the journey outlined in the book? (Circle appropriate answer)

    a. Yes
    b. No

5. How might you/would you have done it differently in retrospect?

Sporting parent challenge

Take a photo / video of your child engaging in their particular sport in their development journey. Upload it on socials and tag @thesportingparent #sportingjourney.

Chapter 8
Elite academies

I was fortunate to have had a few things provided in my childhood. If things were going well for my parents on the business front, they always tried to provide opportunities they might not have had when they were growing up.

One of those opportunities was schooling, and yes, I'm talking about a private school. My parents certainly didn't have everything, but they made sacrifices for us kids to be provided what they felt was an opportunity. Perhaps even slightly better than they had. As with most parents, your mentality could be to provide your kids with better opportunities than you had too, whatever they may be. But it doesn't mean paying for elite academies just for the sake of it.

If you've been around kids' sport long enough, you'll have noticed the rapid rise of elite private academies across Australia. Regardless of the State or suburb where you reside, or the sport you're associated with, they're out there in swarms. In many instances their branding or class time/training slot allocation suggest that *elite* is the game.

If you've discovered one, it might have an ex-player's name associated with it... or even better, if they're coaching there — right?!

Everyone's met that parent whose kid is getting (or has been) coached by player X. This player was a gun back in the day. They were so slick, even dropping their name is bound to leave oil stains.

It only takes a little further delving to realise that athlete X basically had nothing to fall back on when their career finished. Qualifications, degrees, a trade? Nup, nothing!

So, what's the next best thing? Coaching of course! Or athletic development perhaps? Easy — right?! The old adage you'll get heaps of clients because 'everyone knows who you are'.

Forget about the coaches who have been honing their craft during the entire career of athlete X. Your name will trump them all — right?!

For a brief period, yes it will. Until one of two things happen. Firstly, a season or two goes by and no one remembers that cracking goal they kicked or try they scored to finish their career. Or secondly, athlete X comes to the realisation they're simply not passionate about coaching. They find their 'life's calling' promised the world but delivered nothing at all to the innocent parents who gave their hard-earned dollars for their kids to be under athlete X's tutelage.

'It's great to see X in real-estate now, having found his/her life's true calling!', the fans will say.

Let's be honest, if I came out and told you I was going to have a crack at being a professional athlete at age 35 (a retirement age for some — if they make it that far) in any code (take your pick), would you take me seriously? No. You wouldn't... In fact you'd probably tell me I was 'off my head' or 'taking the piss'.

So, am I painting a good picture for you now?...

Either way, you get my vibe but are ex-athlete coaches really everything they're cracked up to be?

The first question I ask is 'are they really an elite coach?'. Prior to enrolling your child and handing over your hard-earned dollars (because let's face it, sport isn't cheap at the best of times), ask the ex-athlete one related question.

'How many of your enrolments have gone on to represent their State, country, or even made it as a professional?'

The definition of elite is 'a select group that is superior in terms of ability or qualities to the rest of a group or society'.[14]

With that definition in mind, I dare say there wouldn't be many (if any). In other words, none. The only thing elite in these settings is the price tag!

Every sport has these elite academies. They're fools gold! I want to be retired at 40 too, driving a Porsche with the house to match and poolside weekend barbecues. But let's be fair-dinkum, we've all seen the bullsh&*t 'get rich quick' schemes... Soon you find yourself asking 'yeah, but what's the catch?'.

If you come from the land of endless opportunity (unlike me or I'm sure many of the parents reading this book), then great. I met plenty of those parents at school too! Seize any opportunity you can and if it means an endless pit of funds — so be it.

But here's the thing... 'Average' doesn't come at a cost — but 'elite' does!

To stay afloat in the business world, products need to be all-year round. If they're not, what business is thriving — right? Unless you're in the business of calendars.

Here's my point — if you ever meet an elite private academy owner who encourages your child to 'come back next season' to work on the extras of their game, holler at me! I'd love to shout the coach a meal — because they'll need it.

I get it, you're either down with me on that 'hell yeah!' vibe right now or your blood is boiling and you're already thinking WTF does this bloke know anyway?

Oh wait, it gets better if you're a coach who's feeling like I'm talking to you… Sorry, not sorry! 😊

If you're following the flow of this book as an empowered sporting parent by now, there's a gentle head nod and your rationalising — 'you know what — it makes sense'.

Some of you are spewing though, I get it.

But let me shed some insights into that 'year-round' CEO parenting forecast that other parents (not you, a sporting parent) have spent sleepless nights chipping away at.

Firstly, as I explained in chapter 6, some sports may require year-round participation for mastery to occur….. *in due course*. The extent of time committed to them can vary, and even support participation in other sports (remember sport sampling?). However, the majority of sports should allow time for you and your child to explore other opportunities and skill sets.

This should be your goal as an informed sporting parent throughout your child's development stages. And you know what? The good development coaches in this space will be nodding their head in agreement and encouraging it. Because they know it's not about the money but the well-being of your child and that it's your child's success (and yours as a sporting parent) that makes them such a successful developmental coach.

After all, isn't that what the majority of sports can benefit from, a multi-skilled athlete? Remember those fundamental movement skills? Why would you sabotage your child's likelihood of success not only via their participation in a specific sport all-year round at the exclusion of others, but also fork over your hard-earned dollars in the process?!...

For bragging rights at the pub about athlete X?

Training year-round in isolation isn't the answer for building resilient and skilful youth. Exploration of sports is. So, no matter how much an elite academy sings this 'year-round training in isolation' chorus, it shouldn't be on your playlist!

I get it, you may have found that 'gem' academy… and even found a relevant place for it in your child's journey. If I'm completely honest, I too have stumbled across the odd diamond glistening in the rough — but they're few and far between.

If you're a wound-up coach fuming about what you've read in this chapter and thinking *'I'll see you when I see you'*, chill. You could very well be one of those gems!

Chapter 9
Understanding the hierarchy of schools, institutes and sporting bodies

There's no doubt about it. When it comes to organisational structures and your child's sporting endeavours within them, it becomes convoluted. Not because these organisations each provide you with a welcome pack highlighting the intricacies of their product, but because much of what they provide is unwritten. Lessons are learnt/acquired through your child's sporting experiences along the way. And each child (and each child's journey) is different.

As a sporting parent, how do you navigate your way through this world to gain a real understanding of how each organisation works? How is the organisation relative to your child's sport? Are each of them necessary for you to achieve success with your child's journey?

You can do one of four things.

Firstly, you can remain quiet, enjoy the journey and simply be content that your child may have the opportunity to be selected in such places of assistance.

Secondly, you can query your inner sanctum of advisors whose kids have been there before in your associated sport. A biased opinion.

Thirdly, you can attack with that CEO mindset already knowing the path that is likely to set your child up for success on their journey... because no one knows a good spreadsheet like you do. Right?! 😉

Or finally you can strap yourself in with your notepad in hand and cut loose on the information I'm about to tell you. It makes sense... I'm a practitioner who's worked among them all. I've been extremely fortunate to have experienced the schooling system in both government and private systems. I've also had multiple relationships with various institutes and sporting bodies throughout my working life.

The one thing they all have in common (despite what you might think) is that they all have your child's best interest at heart. Here's why.

School systems

These are often the first point of contact your child will experience for athletic development/strength and conditioning. The beauty here is there is less pressure and the ability to 'generalise' sports is rarely questioned. For the most part, school should be one of the most positive influences on your child's athletic/personal development and sporting journey.

Whilst school systems are generally still very much in their athletic development infancy (meaning that not every school has a gym), the tide is rapidly turning. When combined with facilities or the quality of coaches, the school context for your child's sporting development should not be overlooked!

Schools are no longer spaces for retired/washed-up, professional journeymen performance coaches to kick their heels up on a comfortable (and most importantly stable) retirement plan!

They are very influential spaces and many schools are rapidly acknowledging their 'niche'. They understand that hiring the right coach is crucial. A coach equipped with enthusiasm, a passion for youth, and enough experience in the development space to know what it takes to succeed.

The biggest challenge for those working in the school athlete development space is twofold. Firstly, they are always the first to get ditched at the slightest sniff of success for a child. Secondly, the jersey more often than not isn't strong enough for your adolescent to truly respect it until later in life!

Then there's the odd parent (not sporting parents like you), who will try and dictate their child's needs because they are going to be 'the next big thing'. (I have been told this on more than one occasion!).

Chapter 9 Understanding the hierarchy of schools, institutes and sporting bodies

It's important to embrace this school time of exploration with your child. Not only is it the most crucial time, but with a bit of success it may be the last time they can actually train/participate in their sport with their school friendship circle (now that's winning right there!).

Did I mention them being exposed to additional positive role models at a very influential time?... Well I just did. 😊

But how do you measure the success of an athletic development program in the high school setting? Simple. Not the championships won, undefeated seasons completed or the institutes/representative club teams its students make. There are two success metrics.

1. Those students who remain physically active for life! I know, right? But there is a big chance your child isn't going to make it professionally. In fact, the vast majority don't. So, is it a bad outcome that your child enjoys training, understands the process and continues to stay active throughout life? The biggest compliments I've ever been given are from several ex-students... 'Sir, you're the reason we still hit the gym! Do you remember X? Without you, time at school would've been ...'

2. If they do progress through the ranks, being physically prepared with accomplished fundamental movement skills and the least amount of limitations. A performance coach in the professional environment can recognise which pathway an athlete came through because of how prepared/equipped they are to progress.

I suppose you're now vibing that schools are one of the most positive influences on your child's athletic development/personal sporting journey???... You should be.

Institutes

The reality with sporting organisations is that funding plays a big part. Not all sports are created equal (and some sports aren't even on the funding radar at your State-based institute/academy of sport etc., unless Australian athletes are considered realistic chances of winning Olympic medals in them).

By 'equal' I also mean the face-to-face coaching contact your child/teen may receive. The greater the funding of a particular sport, the better resources and coaching contact your child is likely to have — from strength and conditioning to physiotherapy, sports psychology and dietetics. Like taxes, unfortunately it is what it is and you don't get a say.

Depending on what school your child has come from, an institute/academy of sport may be the first contact they have with athletic development and what it takes to accomplish athletic success. This further highlights the importance of the school system, irrespective of State/Territory where you live in Australia. The reason comes down to *training age*.

Training age is the time spent in a formally structured training program, usually referred to in years. This age gives coaches a good indication of what your child's movement competency should be.

There's those fundamental movement skills again (eyeroll)…

For example, if a year 9 student has participated in a high school strength and conditioning program (even at a minor level), they would have an approximate training age of 1-2 years (allowing for the ebb and flow of them committing, then not, and then getting inspired again).

Chapter 9 Understanding the hierarchy of schools, institutes and sporting bodies

Some quality high schools around the country even offer programs from year 7! Strength and conditioning training is not what you think or what it was like 'when you grew up'. Resistance training won't stunt your child's growth. Nor will it turn little Mary green or result in her outgrowing her clothes at a rapid rate and looking as vascular as the incredible Hulk! (I'll talk more about resistance training in the next chapter).

If your child hasn't had such a school training opportunity and has been recently selected to join their relevant sporting institute, they are more likely to have a training age of 0 years.

An even playing field? (Pun intended). I think not! But here lies the problem... parental financial struggle means that some kids have had development opportunities while others haven't.

This is particularly challenging for coaching staff at institutes because coach-to-athlete ratios (once again due to funding struggles) often result in athletes at different development levels being grouped together. This under-values any previous quality school training experience your child may have had, purely for simplicity. As a coach, I get it!

Another factor to consider if your child is selected for an institute is that while the offer shouldn't be taken lightly and should be very much appreciated, the institute may not be the best pathway in your child's sport. I'll leave that up to you to decide.

Historically, some sports may have been a part of a State sporting institute only for its national sport-specific organisation to subsequently take 'ownership'. For example, Tennis Australia now hires their own coaches and uses their own athlete development systems/models rather than relying on State sporting institutes. This approach gives organisations like Tennis Australia better control of what is being implemented in their athlete development programs, as well as allowing them to directly allocate/distribute their sport-specific funds (vs. sharing funding across several sports within institutes).

However, many sports are adopting a decentralised model. This creates the opportunity for athletes to fall between the cracks and use local clubs, practitioners and coaching staff to service their needs, even if they're on an institute scholarship.

This has been a common occurrence in Australia since the Sydney 2000 Olympics. Ever wonder what the Australian Institute of Sport (AIS) is being used for now? In some instances, in-house camps with a limited time frame where athletes have access to the luxury of services, facilities and coaching support staff (such as strength and conditioning coaches). Outside of those times, the athletes return to their sport's governing body or their decentralised local clubs. The large, live-in model that the AIS once primarily used is a rarity these days for most athletes.

Sporting bodies

Whether it be the development pathways of a professional sporting team or the national sporting organisation for a particular sport… once again funding is crucial. Having experienced both of them, I will say that both are genuinely supportive in trying to get the best out of kids. For some, it's even in their very best interests to do so given that they too will be a beneficiary of your child's success. The only hurdle is a lack of resources.

I'm showing my age here. If I had a dollar for every time I heard a parent say

Chapter 9 Understanding the hierarchy of schools, institutes and sporting bodies

'It's bloody (insert your favourite sporting club/national sporting organisation here), surely they have enough for X, Y, or Z,' I certainly wouldn't be coaching anymore!

... The reality is they simply don't.

One thing's for certain in this instance. The *jersey* of a professional club will carry weight in your child's peer groups or extended circles — you may even notice a bit more swagger in your son's walk when he wears it. Even an eye roll or two from Daddy's little girl too. 😉

Unfortunately, due to limited funds (which results in less coaching staff and time to invest in each child specifically), once again any previous school and/or institute/State training your child may have had may go unnoticed in this environment.

Then there's the money side of sport and your child. This may be your first exposure to the murky side of sport where your little baby is seen as a commodity and depending on their forecast success (and by that I don't mean the forecasts of your child's team mates or CEO parents, but rather those of experienced talent scouts), financial dealings may take place.

In certain suburbs around the country, a new free pair of boots or the latest running shoes may just persuade little (enter the next big thing's name here)'s judgement of who his/her favourite team is again. ☺

The bottom line

The reality is that in the development stages, sport and your child's participation in it is paramount. The proportion of time you commit and encourage your child to focus on in a particular sport throughout the year is up to you.

Don't forget the importance of the schooling influence… What? It's free too you say! (well inclusive anyway).

Just remember to ask yourself this question the next time you're going to question the funding allocation of your favourite sporting club, governing body or national sporting organisation — prior to your child's selection, what have you done as a sporting parent to adequately prepare them?

Chapter 9 Understanding the hierarchy of schools, institutes and sporting bodies

Think Box

Calculating Training Age

Training age = total number of years participating in a formal/structured strength and conditioning program

- Does (or has) your child participate(d) in a structured strength and conditioning program?   Yes / No

- If you answered Yes', estimate the total time spent (allowing for dropping out times or seasonal transitions). What is the total time in years? _____

Lesson from the Field #3
Belinda Carpenter

Belinda Carpenter is one of those gems. Belinda along with her now ex-husband Scott has raised two children (now young adults, Jeremy and Ellie) to play professional sport (football), but to be two quality humans who are also likely to positively contribute to society as well.

Originally from Cowra in country NSW, the family would travel over 200 kilometres per weekly trip to ensure both Jeremy and Ellie were provided with the best opportunity to succeed. In many instances, this would mean leaving work/school early at 2pm to ensure both Jezz and Ellie made it to training by

6pm. Then to pack up and commence the trip home at 8pm, sometimes arriving back home as late as 1am. If that's not commitment, I don't know what is!

Like many young Australian footballers, Jeremy had to apply his craft the best way he knew how in the overseas market. By 15 he was experiencing a new culture in Japan, at 17 he was learning a new language in Portugal at FB Belenenses and then Oliveira Do Bairro, before eventually landing himself in Germany for Borussia Lindenthal-Hohenlind. He returned home in 2019 to face the exciting prospect of commencing a science degree in 2021.

Ellie debuted for the national team (the Matildas) at 15. She was the youngest athlete to represent Australia at the 2016 Rio Olympics and the youngest footballer to ever compete at an Olympic games. Ellie continues to represent her country and play professionally overseas. At the time of writing, Ellie is playing for Olympique Lyonnais in France.

What roles did schooling, institutes or sporting bodies play for your kids coming through the ranks?

Back when Jezz and Ellie started out, Football NSW had a program known as 'Project 22'. It was made very clear when signing the contract that they weren't permitted under any circumstances to train with an outside academy.

It was a challenging time because while they started out in Project 22, eventually both were fortunate to become enrolled at Westfields Sports High School.

Both had requirements to uphold to ensure they kept their positions. This became problematic because in a worst-case scenario they may have ended up playing a match for school that day, and then there was extreme pressure to perform in a match that night!

Coming from the country, we were a little naïve in trying to follow exact protocol... for a certain period of time. I don't think either the school or Football NSW necessarily factored each other into their training programs. At times this was very challenging. Given they were both separate entities and my kids were expected to perform for both of them regardless, we had to become resourceful in making it work and managing their training and playing loads.

We had to think bigger picture and adopt perhaps a less orthodox approach.

Sometimes we would focus on their recovery rather than them going to school. When there may have been a game one day and another the following night, we had to adopt a strategy with a clear and conscious focus on recovery for the following game. Whether that was going to the beach for a walk or swim in the water — that was just what we had to do.

I don't know if one (school or institute) was necessarily better than the other. Both provided exceptional technical coaching opportunities. We just happened to benefit being a part of both, combined with meeting exceptional coaches who guided us along the way.

What did you as a sporting parent feel was the natural pathway to success in football?

Both kids played any sport they could in Cowra. That was just the way it was. Kids just came from anywhere to fill a team. They both got selected for their regional teams, and I'd heard of this Project 22. So I actually called the convener who coordinated Western Football and asked, 'Why aren't we in this?'. There were plenty of country kids who would have been happy to be in it!

Eventually there were kids from Dubbo, Parkes, Forbes, Young and Cowra given the opportunity. All would have to travel to one centre twice a week. Some of us would be travelling 100–200 kilometres+ per session. That was just to train!

Then we would have to travel to Sydney on the weekends to play against the city kids.

That changed when Jezz was invited into the metropolitan program. Things followed on from there.

Originally there were no girls in Project 22. In fact, the very first camp Ellie attended as a 9 year old, they thought 'she' was Eli (a he)… until this little blonde girl with pig-tails turned up! They frantically rushed around to get a female coach involved. Funnily enough the same coach ended up being Ellie's U/13 State coach.

To ensure Ellie was given every opportunity, I looked up the constitution to find it only stated 'player'. We wrote to the crew at Western Region and so eventually they let her play!

Ellie was playing the metropolitan league in Sydney and was the only girl playing. It was great! Because then eventually Project 22 started to get other girls in her age group as well.

This was an amazing step forward in football, not only for Ellie but for other girls in the State too.

For us, the pathway originally came out of Project 22. So I suppose you could say Football NSW was their first exposure to quality coaching and competition. The schooling came next. I wouldn't necessarily say there was a distinct pathway as such, but there were a handful of exceptional people at Football NSW along the way that had our back.

Load became a massive issue for both my kids. With Project 22, school and premier league — which were all prerequisites of each other — it was immense! As a matter of fact, at the time they were still doing other sports such as athletics, touch and anything else that was playing at the time. Like any other Australian kids do!

We then had to sit down and really think about which way we were going to go. Remember you're talking 9 and 10-year old kids here.

Both were very different in stature and ability. Jezz was a late developer and while athletic, more of a technical player. We decided it was better for him to head to Japan down the track.

As a family we are very much 'can-do' people. Take a punt, take a risk! But living something can be very different to what you may have expected it to be. Living overseas by the time he was 15, with a different language and culture while still being a kid was extremely challenging for Jezz. Throw in our family treading through its own issues at the time, and it was an extremely challenging and character-building time in his life! One that I don't think he was necessarily prepared for at that time.

Ellie stayed here for just that little bit longer. Approximately 18 months longer, but she went overseas with the Olympic team, flying off here and there, but I just felt like she would still come home. Whereas Jezz couldn't. While it's shaped the amazing person he is today, from a footballer's perspective it may have been a bit too early.

I can't prove that because Ellie was already in the system where she was better off. But what I can say is that whatever path you take, you own the decision and wear the consequences. Just because you go and spend money to send your child overseas to give them an opportunity or different perspective, it doesn't mean they're guaranteed a professional contract or likely to be the next Cristiano Ronaldo — it just doesn't!

One thing is for certain — there's no guarantee for any of the paths you take!

As a sporting parent, where did you draw your information from? As in where did you look to make decisions in both their journeys?

I didn't know anything about football. Anything! I'm from an athletics background and would have been happy if they'd pursued that. But both preferred team sports and I supported them. I promised them if you guys get selected in this or that, we'll move.

That was that. We moved. And things became a bit more serious then. Jezz was 12 years old starting high school and Ellie was still in primary school.

I left my job and sold our home — so in other words, we left everything. As a parent you're now investing everything and you don't do that unless you educate yourself. I looked and listened to every other player in a higher age group who we thought was good and then Jezz, Ellie and I would watch them play. What made them different? What avenue were they taking to separate themselves from others? Was it outside coaching? What school were they at? Are they in this team or that?

Both Jezz and Ellie were athletic. They didn't necessarily need help with that. But we had to be on a mission to find that technical opportunity in football! Because we never had that opportunity in Cowra... we didn't even know what futsal was! They had never been exposed to indoor soccer and things like that.

I spent countless hours sitting in the grandstands and listening to the various Dads. All were from various backgrounds around the world and they clearly knew far more about football than I did.

I then sought help. If it was from coaches I'd ask, 'What if we hung around training for a little while longer?' Paid or not — it didn't matter. We had three or so coaches who contributed in some capacity. It was a reciprocal relationship. Because we were dedicated to going, they would commit their time to us.

Do you have any advice for new sporting parents that you wish you knew earlier on?

It has nothing to do with the football. It's the emotional toll it took in navigating the system and working out which people are good for you or not. Not just to increase my kids' skills or abilities but their mental or emotional health. The ability to recognise what a good person in that environment for them would be. Those who genuinely cared.

I personally have kept to myself. If I don't understand something, I ask.

For Jezz, things were a bit more experimental. Because we were so new and not from a football background, there was plenty of trial and error. Acknowledging that things don't always go your way and we certainly got a few things wrong. You don't have all the doors open just when you want them!

For Ellie, there was a year and a half difference in age. With a little more experience and knowledge, our decisions became clearer. We also became wiser to various people's actions in helping us — not just words! At Project 22 we were very fortunate to have met an exceptional human who was able to mentor us on a specific path. He was very clear about how and on what stage Ellie needed to perform to be identified and selected for certain teams.

One thing is very clear — if either of my kids were on the bench, the coach put them there for a reason. I don't ask, I don't get involved, and I don't get involved with the other parents. These things are always going to happen and you can't control them.

My kids and I would never ask why they weren't getting played. I wouldn't even encourage them to ask. As a parent it was my role to say to my kids, 'What are you going to do about it?!'.

I have always told them 'you are in control of what you're doing'. You make sure of your preparation and that you're ready… all the time. Then, and only then, if the time comes and you don't agree with a decision — then we go around them. Never through people. Everyone is entitled to their opinion and I would never question that. It's not my right to do so.

But what we could do is find another way. Change our path. We never tried to prove others wrong. It's just a waste of energy!

As a sporting parent, if you see potential nurture it. If your child is not getting themselves up in the morning, waiting with their boots on at 5am, then they don't want it! If you have to wake them up to get them to training or to get them going — they don't want it!

How would you define success as a sporting parent for your family now that your kids are adults?

Having dabbled in a variety of sports throughout their childhood, we knew if they wanted to make something out of sport — Sydney was the benchmark. In one particular camp Jezz was awarded one of three prizes out of 80 kids. We thought we might actually be OK at this!

From that day on, we always said you have to know what you're capable of. Regardless of others' opinions. We actually termed this 'rate or hate'. It doesn't matter if someone rates you or hates you, as long as you as an individual know what you can do!

Prizes, awards and accolades don't define who or what you are, and they don't define what you feel you can achieve. Motivation is very much intrinsic in both my kids, not extrinsic.

Intrinsic motivation has to start when they're young. If it only comes from validation or receiving something, you can't sustain that!

The biggest success both my kids had is in overcoming adversity — because we had a lot of things go wrong. My proudest achievement is them not blaming anyone for where they have ended up. Acknowledging where they could have done better as individuals in their career or life and seeking the resources to correct them. Acknowledge and seeking at such young ages is empowering!

They're resilient, practical and grounded. Both have always understood throughout their playing careers (and particularly with Ellie right now), that it's a bubble. She could lose it all tomorrow and acknowledges that she is not purely defined by being Ellie Carpenter the footballer. Neither are owed anything after their careers.

I personally didn't care if they played professional football or not. They wanted to! I just did everything I could to facilitate it.

Chapter 10
The elephant in the room (children and resistance training)

If you were like me and had any interest in sport growing up, your first set of dumbbells were a right of passage. I couldn't wait to save up and get my first pair. If you didn't save up for them, maybe you were given them as a birthday present or maybe they were handed down from your older brother.

However you got them, while you were hiding out in the garage working out and looking in the mirror, your Mum was more than likely fretting. I remember my Mum saying, 'you shouldn't lift weights until you're 16', as clear as day.

I'm not sure which health professional can actually take credit for first saying that, but they deserve to be in the running for a Nobel Prize because parents have been quoting it for decades! It's predecessor, 'lifting weights will stunt your growth', is another that's stood the test of time.

But here's the thing — if you're a parent using either of those sayings, I call bullust!

Chapter 10   The elephant in the room (children and resistance training)

As I highlighted in chapter 4, our youth of today are extremely underprepared for the rigours of sport, largely due to their lack of physical activity. For bones to become strong and healthy, they need to be compressed and contorted in different ways. This often occurs naturally through things like running, jumping and various other locomotor movements during sport.

If our youth are significantly challenged in essential fundamental movement skills, it's no wonder they're crumbling like chalk.

...Whoops, do they still even use chalk? No — largely due to skin and/or respiratory allergies (funnily enough). Is there anything our precious little cherubs aren't allergic to these days?

Don't believe me? Google *'paediatric dynapenia'* and see what comes up. It's scary to think our youth of today are on par with our grandparents when it comes to physical ailments/conditions that prevent them from completing simple day-to-day tasks.

Scoff as you may... but remember — *we* created this generation.

But do you know the antidote to this treatable condition? Strength training!

Research has shown that regular participation by youth (children/adolescents) in resistance training has a positive effect on fundamental movement skills (running, jumping and throwing).[15]

Take a moment to reflect back on your child's performance in the fundamental movement tests in chapter 4. How did they go? Did they perform like you expected?

If their performance wasn't up to scratch, it reinforces that they need to improve their fundamental movement skills. Combined with an increased likelihood of injury as a result of their limited exposure to physical activity, what's the solution?

Once again...strength training. Here are the several reasons why.

Increased bone mineral density

Bones strengthen when they are contorted in various ways under what we 'meatheads' call 'load'. In other words, additional weight. The additional weight doesn't have to be the latest and greatest equipment. It can simply be body weight. Load combined with movement encourages bones to bend or twist, which in turn encourages remodelling. Combined with the maturation process, this remodelling will strengthen your child's bones. A major outcome is injury prevention. No more fractures! 😊

Chapter 10 The elephant in the room (children and resistance training)

Enhanced physical literacy

If our youth are lacking in physical activity, what better way to increase their participation rates than through resistance training? It may provide that additional exercise variety to stimulate and challenge them. The by-product... enhanced physical literacy and fundamental movement skills (again).

A good strength program is not only about load, it challenges movement in a variety of different 'planes'. Simply translated, a strength program should be multi-directional and include both upper and lower body variations.

... No! It's not about how much your child can bench press. Or how many bicep curls per week they can complete.

Hence why hubby's program that got him big and strong just won't cut it. Neither will Little Sally's older brother's magazine-based program (oh wait, they're cookie-cutter online programs these days!).

It's also not a right of passage to enter into the domain of supplement use for your child at the mere sniff of resistance training (but more on that in the next chapter).

Strengthened supportive tissues

A special thing happens when muscles contract and relax under additional load. The supportive tissues (like tendons) also remodel. That's it, a two-for-one offer. A buy-one, get- one free. The same goes for additional jumping, hopping or any other moderate-to-high-intensity exercise.

What are the outcomes you might ask? Simple… Think back to chapter 3 (the physical cost of technology and potential hospital bills). Not only are fractures a concern when kids have a lack of physical activity, but dislocations are another. Strengthening ligaments may just help prevent that shoulder or knee complication in future.

I couldn't write a book like this without at least mentioning the dreaded anterior cruciate ligament (ACL) once or twice. It's every athlete's worst nightmare, even more so in professional sport.

While resistance training won't eliminate the possibility of an ACL injury from occurring, it may just help prevent it. Combined with increased physical literacy, you're simply bullet proofing!

Decreased likelihood of injury

Well, enough said!

Chapter 10 The elephant in the room (children and resistance training)

Promote healthier lifelong choices

I mentioned this in the previous chapter when discussing schooling environments — healthier lifelong choices is one of the biggest determinants of success in your child's sporting journey. In fact it's proven. Various fitness parameters such as strength developed in childhood promote healthier outcomes later in life![16]

Exercise variety (such as resistance training) encourages your child to not only understand the benefits associated with various methods of exercise, it also provides further opportunity for it to be enjoyed.

More enjoyment = greater adherence.

Our youth of today already have enough self-acceptance challenges. Instagram feeds are filled with jacked-up, bikie-looking fellas or young girls with enough silicone or Botox to put Pamela Anderson to shame. Body dysmorphia is a real thing, and it's a big thing with our youth of today in particular! Gaining more self-acceptance and confidence through resistance training may well be an ingredient to encourage their healthier life-long choices.

So, while the urban myth that 'strength training will hurt our youth' is likely to continue — as a sporting parent, be the difference! Support your child's development rather than hinder it.

Lesson from the Field #4
Lachlan Wilmot

Lachlan Wilmot is a juggernaut in the world of athletic development. From having coached some of the country's finest athletes through the development pathway into professional AFL via the Greater Western Sydney (GWS) Giants to being head of performance for the Parramatta Eels in the NRL to now being a co-owner of the premier private athlete performance facility in Australia — Athletes Authority.

Lachie understands what it takes to transition through the younger development stages and how to prepare athletes at the top of their pedigree.

Growing up as a kid in Australia, when did you first pick up a dumbbell or barbell and start strength training?

I was fortunate to be a part of a family actively involved in the fitness industry. Both my Mum and sister were personal trainers. Combined with being introduced to sport early, I was also a very early developer. I was quite a sizeable kid. At first a little overweight. I used to get teased in my younger years in primary school.

I discovered early that there were sports where size was an advantage. From centre back in football to ruckman in AFL, using my size against my opponents. Around Year 5 and 6 I discovered that while I was strong, I was relatively unfit. I began going for runs around the streets myself. Both My mum and sister helped me out with running.

Chapter 10 The elephant in the room (children and resistance training)

I started traditional strength training when I started high school in Year 7. We had a home gym and my sister's boyfriend at the time was an avid bodybuilder. He helped me get on my way. Already training two to three times per week, it just became my passion.

Plenty of mistakes created invaluable learning experiences. Many of those lessons stay true today. I made every mistake you could think of — from progressing too quickly to understanding what it meant to be sore.

I did everything, progressing from very simple to complex movements. Over time I began to realise that strength training not only supported my strength gains, it encouraged me to trim down and improve my body composition. Given my frame as a young boy, that was definitely a positive.

There were so many benefits I look back on that I can attribute to commencing my strength training. I began to eat better and focus on things I could control to help me get where I wanted to go.

Even with all my Mum's experience over the years, even now she probably thinks weight training stunts your growth. But standing at 6 foot, I'm still taller than your average bloke. To me one of the most common misconceptions of strength training for parents is that it will stunt your child's growth! I certainly had no issues with it stunting my growth.

Given the abundance of research that has come out over the years in support of the benefits of youth strength training, combined with my experience both personally and professionally, we at Athletes Authority are big advocates that the positives far outweigh any potential negatives.

Your former role as Head of Strength and Power at GWS would have been an interesting one. Not only did you get to work with some impressive specimens in the AFL but you were also responsible for building our stars of the future through the development pathway. What are the top strength training concepts that come to mind from the development pathway through to playing or working with senior professional players?

As a coach, the long-term influence you can have on an athlete is multifactorial. Strength training plays a big part in that!

1. Mentality/Attitude

The earlier we got an athlete, the greater influence I had in laying the foundations for a lifetime. Not only from a physical standpoint, but mental as well. We had a big focus early on at the Giants on being strong. In some instances, I was fortunate enough to have players as young as 15 enter our NSW program who have since moved on to other clubs and are now considered senior players in the AFL. It was only upon seeing how far other clubs were behind us from a strength perspective that they realised the benefits of what they'd been a part of at the Giants — how important being strong is and the translation to their overall success.

2. Injury resilience

Whether they'd come from other clubs or we'd inherited them in their early days, players had often had pre-season after pre-season of injury. Discovering what they'd previously been doing incorrectly (or in other instances had overlooked) and addressing that was crucial. Seeing that come to fruition for players at 21 or so and them then playing a full season of AFL was rewarding. A lot of strength coaches will say that when their team is strong, then they're happy. But to be honest, a lot of the times I've seen players the happiest is when they've got through pre-season and actually get to play!

Chapter 10   The elephant in the room (children and resistance training)

Everyone sees the names of players who make it, but they rarely see the names of those who go out the back door without playing a game because they just couldn't get their bodies right! From a developmental standpoint, if they can learn how to do that from an early age (15/16), it's great! Unfortunately, it's all too common that a player gets to 28/29 before realising how important all that stuff is — but they've had to get there to realise that!

3. Routines and habits
In the development space, when players discovered that the little things done outside of football (like habits and routines) produced a dominance on the field that was instrumental to their careers. I still see it all the time. Players may overlook a sleep routine, don't pay attention to the importance of their diet/nutrition, or things are all a bit too random. And
then so is their football! Once they're able to stabilise their external environment and build an effective, consistent routine, they begin to play good footy.

Far too many players underestimate the impact such stability and consistency can have on their training and ultimately playing performance. Strength training plays an important role in building effective habits and routines because to be successful and get what you want to get out of it, players need to consider extrinsic factors.

You're now co-director of the premium athlete performance facility in Australia, Athletes Authority. With countless youth lining up to be a part of your program, how do you view youth strength training today?

We have two programs on offer at Athletes Authority. One is an Emerging Athlete Program (EAP) for 16-year-olds and under. The other is our Athlete Development Program (ADP) which is essentially 16/17-year-olds and beyond.

The whole concept of the Emerging Athlete Program is educating through the training process. Teaching correct movement patterns, understanding what strength is, where mobility comes into play, how to change direction efficiently, if you need more conditioning — the list goes on. All those parameters create a really good athlete. Until you can create a good athlete, there's no point trying to specialise in a particular sport or the training involved with it.

The EAP is supported by research, and as practitioners we know that kids who play multiple sports have different technical and tactical advantages that ultimately help them in the future (except for those rare instances in particular sports like gymnastics where their peak competitive age is far earlier).

Only once we've built an all-encompassing young athlete do we start to delve deeper into particular sports. They then transition into our Athlete Development Program.

As youth start to get to about 16/17 years of age they start to better understand where they want to go with their sport and we start to specialise. A by-product is that we then begin to individualise various training parameters to a greater depth.

Unfortunately, a lot of coaches tend to over-specialise because they want to prove themselves in the athletic development space. Good athletic development coaches believe in what they're doing and don't try to prove themselves.

There are degrees to which we program strength training to set our athletes up for success. The progressions and regressions we use initially are to build structures and ranges of motion. These ultimately support the path for our athletes as their program becomes more specific with advanced exercises that translate to their sport.

When coaches skip the various degrees of strength training in order to specialise, their athletes become underdeveloped in their capacity to resist injuries from their sport. They eventually break-down and become injured.

Our goal as athletic development coaches is to assist technical coaches (irrespective of the sport) to make their athletes tolerate their training loads (and thus get better at their sport).

If you could give one bit of strength training advice to sporting parents, what would it be?

The youth of today can't simply rely on their technical training or playing the game to improve their strength. From as young as 9 years old (or even earlier) through to 15 and beyond, they need to be participating in a good, strength-based program focusing on movement.

They don't need to be spending 5 days a week in the gym doing bench press!

I would suggest as little as twice a week in an athletic development facility or a gym, focusing on good movement patterns such as squatting, lunging, hinging, pushing and pulling as developmental exercises. They need to be doing and focusing on these capacities as a set session within itself.

You simply can't rely on your sport to get you strong if you want to take it to the next level down the track. Examples would be track and field athletes relying on running to build leg strength. Or footy players focusing on tackling to build upper body strength.

Allowing athletes to build certain capacities before they need them allows them to jump to those more advanced exercises faster as an athlete.

Having recently become a proud father to Briar, will she be participating in strength training and if so, how early?

In short, from my perspective — absolutely! In saying that though — first and foremost it's about fun.

No matter what your aspirations are as a parent, ultimately your child will make the decisions whether you like them or not. All I can do is present her with options, but ultimately she'll be deciding whether she wants to or not.

When it comes to specific strength training, there's no doubt I'll start doing various things with her as soon as she can start moving around. Simple things like kicking or throwing a ball back and forth as soon as she can, as well as picking toys up from the ground and putting them down. People often mistakenly associate strength training with dumbbells — it certainly isn't.

I'm in a gym day to day. She'll be visiting frequently and there will definitely be an element of it rubbing off on her. I've seen it time and time again. When kids are in an environment surrounded by activities, there's an element of it that rubs off on them.

I'll be teaching her how to do correct exercises with the necessary equipment, but it will be a slow evolution of me exposing her to as much variety as I can — from general movement to specific strength work — whichever is more appropriate for her at the time. In the early days, most of it will be introducing her to different sports and making sure that she can make a decision of what she enjoys by herself.

Chapter 11
Supplement use

There's no doubt about it, this is one of the hottest topics in youth sport! Should your child start (or be taking) supplements?

While you may scoff at the initial thought of it, one thing's for certain — if you have a teenage boy, the question's coming. Even little Maggie is going to be knocking down your door wanting to jump on something or another!

Those savvy marketing strategies are tailored to your self-conscious, growing child. Unfortunately, now more than ever. Body image plays a monumental role. Youth are chasing self-approval measured through social media likes and Instagram influencers are flogging products for personal leverage. That skinny detox tea perhaps?

More often than not, supplements are viewed by sporting parents from the perspective of supporting their children to succeed, as opposed to getting an edge over their opponents.

Harmless right? Child's best interest, yeah? Just looking out for your child?

Wrong. Below are several reasons you may have never thought of that will likely hinder rather than encourage your child's future success in sport, and in life!

Instant gratification

You'll hear me say this time and time again. We have created 'this generation'. That's right, we have! Don't complain about their behaviours, interests or motivations without self-reflecting on the impacts your decisions as a parent have had on your child's development and mindset.

As I mentioned in chapter 3, it only seems like yesterday to me that we had a dial-up connection to the internet. You might have been in the midst of an online chat/game when a call came through on the home line and the internet dropped out! (When you answered the phone with 'What?!', Aunty Gretel thought 'moody little prick!'). Then you had to dial up and wait (for what felt like an hour) to reconnect…

Well this generation doesn't! A screen freeze of more than 5 seconds is deemed too slow (hahaha, oh how we forget).

Purchasing supplements for your child encourages instant gratification. It teaches them it's OK to chase instant success. It's normal to get results immediately.

If they don't get it, they'll just move on to the next heavily marketed product to succeed… Damn! At this rate, they probably won't even finish the tub of protein you spent your hard-earned dollars on before they jump ship!

… And we wonder why this generation lacks resilience. That it's OK to throw the towel in because little Johnny got dropped or Maggie was played out of position. Let's face it — that sport's outright sh&*t! Right?

Freedom to choose

Part of the excitement of getting your weekly family take-away meal was probably the ride to (insert your favourite junk food here) fast food chain with your Mum/Dad. Mouth-watering the whole way there, with a firm decision of your order etched into your brain. Only to be stumped at the drive-through by second guessing yourself…. Argh! I should've gone with X!

…. What about the drink spills on the car ride home? Or the many dropped drink holders trying to juggle everyone's 'jumbo' drinks while getting out of the car on a hot summer's night?! Sh&*t! (Again).

If you were like me, you were trying to steal your brother or sister's better order. If not the entire order, at least elements of it! A nugget here or there with a 'What's that?' (pointing to distract attention) and then boom!

Well that choice doesn't even come close to the variety available to our youth of today (I did say 'our' because 'we' have the choice to shape their future). Jeez, they can even order food while sitting on the couch and have someone deliver it to them!

As a parent, you open the door to an infinite number of choices by purchasing and encouraging your child's supplement use. Combined with instant gratification, there's only one option left... an endorsement deal! Because you won't have any cash left to support your child's new-found gateway to accomplish sporting success.

… And yet again we wonder why they can't 'stick' to a sport or show the 'commitment' we did in our day!

Performance anxiety

Every athlete wants to do their best. The more experienced they get, the greater preparation goes into just that. The process.

When little Johnny/or Maggie has taken X consistently before a number of training sessions or games/matches, it becomes a habit. Habitually they not only take a supplement product but are likely to win (preferably) or perform well as a result.

So, what happens when that product runs out? Or they forget it, along with their boots?

You're nodding your head now having flashbacks driving all the way home as you've arrived at a venue only to have your child ask the dreaded 'Where are my boots?!' question.

While a physical dependence on supplements isn't very likely, a psychological one could well be realistic.

Performance anxiety is normal. But what about anxiety knowing you may not be able to perform in the absence of X? That just adds another dimension to the already very complex world of kids' sport!

The best outcome… simply never trying it in the first place.

Education

The best part of working in the youth space is watching them learn along the way. That's right, actually learning and digesting the information. It's the most rewarding part of my job as a coach. It genuinely excites me! 😊

This generation is encouraged to seek answers immediately like no other ever has before! The difference is this — while they have every answer at the click of a button (or search engine), any professional in the educational space will tell you that they often don't have the ability to actually understand that information.

… So yes, they do have the world at their feet, but sling them your latest 'Gregory's' in the absence of a device and watch them navigate their way home! They'll have next to zero idea of what to do (hahaha — harsh, but fair).

Then again, when are they ever going to be without access to a device? If you don't wonder that yourself, then they'll certainly be throwing it back at your wise parenting advice.

Part of the journey as a sporting parent is encouraging your child to respect 'the process'. This doesn't happen by you telling them or even sharing your 'war stories' as a youth. It happens by placing them in an environment that encourages them to display their understanding.

It's the situations you place your child in that allows them to think, react and retain information that will likely support their sporting success down the track… Not what you tell them.

For example — 'What is a good source of protein? When would be the best time for you to have it? How would you go about taking it to your local athletics track, football field or tennis complex? Would you prepare it? How would it remain chilled?

The bottom line

Supplement use is an expensive, unnecessary (in the majority of cases) and convoluted exercise that will not necessarily encourage your child's sporting success, but even hinder it — and perhaps their life too!

Lesson from the Field #5
Health and Performance Collective

Health and Performance Collective is an authority in the dietetic space. It was created by Chloe McLeod and Jessica Spendlove, both accredited, practising dietitians and advanced sports dietitians specialising in performance nutrition.

Health and Performance Collective has a proven track record in harnessing professional athletes and teams across multiple sports. Its Sydney-based team works with motivated people throughout Australia — both online and face-to-face — to help them not only to live but to perform at their best.

With 31 seasons of professional sport (and counting), some of Health and Performance Collective's teams include:

- GWS Giants (AFL)
- Parramatta Eels (NRL)
- Cronulla Sharks (NRL)
- South Sydney Rabbitohs (NRL)
- Western Sydney Wanderers (A-League)
- Sydney Kings (NBL)
- NSW Waratahs (Super Rugby)
- Roxsolt Attaquer (cycling)
- Carlile Swimming.

I'll cut to the chase — in the majority of instances, do our youth of today require the use of supplements?

The most simple answer here is 'no'. The use of supplements with the specific goal of performance enhancement is both unwanted and hazardous in adolescence. Adolescent athletes are likely to find greater performance gains through:

- experience and maturation in their sport,

- encouraging them to find the joy and 'fun' in their sport,

- supporting their activity through making great nutrition choices, and

- ensuring adequate rest (this is forgotten way too often!).

Excessive focus on body composition, particularly through use of supplements that encourage 'mass gains' and leanness (hey there skinny teas...!) aren't just concerning at this impressionable age, they can be down right dangerous. It can be tough as a parent these days, when having a protein powder in the cupboard is as common as having a jar of peanut butter — no wonder it can be so hard to know what is actually OK and what isn't!

Parents' nutritional goal should be to encourage adolescent habits and choices that build a strong, life-long foundation for both health and performance.

It is the role of the parent to support adolescent nutrition choices that both encourage and reinforce long-term health, positive body image and a positive relationship with food. Not to support apparent gains by cutting corners and using dodgy supplements.

But it's important to note the difference between a performance supplement and a dietary supplement. For example, iron is a common dietary supplement which may be required if an individual's iron levels are low.

It's also important to note that while the above may sound very 'anti-supplement', it's certainly not the case. Supplements have their place and their uses. But they should be used in appropriate scenarios as just that, supplements, not replacements.

We encourage parents who are unsure to get expert advice via reaching out to an accredited sports dietitian.

What are the biggest nutritional challenges facing our youth of today

- Competition — of course your kid wants to be the best, to find that 'edge'. Unfortunately that 'edge' is not always what will be best for them long term and helping them understand that can be challenging.
- Comparison — being compared to your peers is difficult at any age, but none more so than during the teenage years.
- Media messages — the media has a lot to answer for, particularly when it comes to body image issues.

Have you got a story from hell or a cringeworthy example of any particular client's poor nutrition/strategy?

A few spring to mind:

- a parent with a teenager who participated in MMA, where body composition is very important. Unfortunately the teenager had also been diagnosed with an eating disorder. The parent was more concerned about getting the kid to the next comp and winning a medal than about managing his mental health and supporting him through this challenging condition.

- a parent whose child was on track to make it to the highest level in their sport. Unfortunately this teenager was tall and lean, and needed to gain size to 'make it'. The parent (regardless of advice) had put the kid on a strict regime of supplements to achieve that. Sure, the child gained size, but I have since heard they have also injured themselves so badly there is no chance they'll 'make it'. Was it worth it?

- a parent putting a child on a vegan diet, though he actually didn't want to be. Considering this child's individual nutrition requirements and those of his sport, without correct implementation the risk of deficiencies and loss of muscle mass is high. By the time I saw him, he had already lost a significant amount of muscle, was constantly sick and finding it difficult to recover effectively. While there's nothing wrong with a vegan diet, it should be implemented correctly using quality produce. Forcing beliefs onto your children is also highly questionable.

Are there any strategies/examples you know of where companies are strategically targeting youth in the supplement game?

Unfortunately, yes. One company has their 'Young Athlete Protein' while another has their 'Kids Complete' range.* These supplements prey on young peoples' insecurities and encourage the use of products they likely don't need in order to provide instant gratification, or 'success'.

While in certain instances high-energy and protein drinks may be required to support adolescents and children with higher energy needs or who find it difficult to consume enough due to allergies/intolerances, the majority of adolescents won't require these products. These products are marketed as more of a sports supplement.

Our main concern is that it can be easy for unwanted substances to appear in products because the supplement industry is so poorly regulated. We think it's important that young people (all people really!) learn how to make healthy food choices to support their daily lives and performance needs before starting to rely on supplements.

* It should be noted that at the time of writing, we have been made aware that Sports Dietitians Australia is working with both companies to address the promotion and use of these products.

What are the top three strategies to ensure youth are adequately prepared to endure the demands of their current sport, irrespective of the playing level?

- Adequate nutritional intake to support their training, development and growth.

  This can be achieved through the use of real, quality food. Get your kid involved in the shopping and the cooking. Make your breakfast smoothies together. Help them learn how great they feel after eating enough prior to a training session, and how much better they recover when they have made great choices afterwards.

  Getting the nutrition piece right at this age can have long-term health implications in every aspect of their life, including their relationship with food, how tall they grow, how strong their bones get, and everything in between.

- Training regimes that do not encourage overtraining.

- Rest/sleep.

  This one is too often forgotten, but it's where the magic really happens.

Chapter 12
What does development/maturation mean?

Youth growth and maturation is not without its challenges for sport. Just like a good business, every child will go through peaks and troughs in their journey. Some will *appear* less impacted throughout adolescence than others.

… I did say 'less impacted' because after reading this chapter you'll understand the challenges every child faces. Yours is no different. 😊

I think at some stage every parent wonders why their child may look overpowered, slower, or like they lack the ability to hit the mark with ball sports.

Here's the thing — gaining a better understanding of the maturation process and how it's likely to impact your child's success in sport is crucial. This understanding may even support your decision to choose particular sports for your child.

As a sporting parent, by now you're understanding and even accepting that your child playing multiple sports is going to be beneficial, especially in the long term.

So, what if certain sports at the right time were better than others in building your child's athletic prowess? Would you explore them? Who knows, maybe after reading this chapter you'll think differently.

Remember that delayed gratification we spoke about in Chapter 3...

The reality is this — the more time you devote to looking into the most idealistic training model for your child, the deeper the rabbit hole you're going to fall into. The best advice I can shed on this topic is 'it's not their fault!'... As in your child's, because let's remember it's about them — not those projected forecasts of CEO parents.

The best decisions you can make in your child's sporting journey are adaptive. As we all did during the COVID-19 pandemic — pivot. Some did it better than others. As a sporting parent, it's no different.

The most realistic supported evidence I can provide for you from my experience is the Youth Physical Development Model.[17] While it may look complicated, it's super easy to interpret.

The main reason why I particularly like this model is that it highlights one thing. Clearly. Whether you have a boy, a girl or both, it highlights there are changes that take place. And that both genders develop at different times. Simple.

So easy in fact, you'll be a wizard panning over it with a sneaky coffee awaiting the start of your regular Saturday morning fixture.

Basically — the larger the font and more prominently coloured the region, the greater the emphasis on the particular physical parameter... there you go, easy! They have even separated boys from girls for you (blue and pink)...

Chapter 12 What does development/maturation mean?

YOUTH PHYSICAL DEVELOPMENT (YPD) MODEL FOR MALES

CHRONOLOGICAL AGE (YEARS)	2	3	4	5	6	7	8	9	10	11	12	13	14	15	16	17	18	19	20	21+
AGE PERIODS	EARLY CHILDHOOD			MIDDLE CHILDHOOD						ADOLESCENCE								ADULTHOOD	
GROWTH RATE	RAPID GROWTH ↔ STEADY GROWTH ↔ ADOLESCENT SPURT ↔ DECLINE IN GROWTH RATE																				
MATURATIONAL STATUS	YEARS PRE-PHV ← PHV → YEARS POST-PHV																				
TRAINING ADAPTATION	PREDOMINANTLY NEURAL (AGE-RELATED) ↔ COMBINATION OF NEURAL AND HORMONAL (MATURITY-RELATED)																				

PHYSICAL QUALITIES:
- FMS | FMS | FMS | FMS
- SSS | SSS | SSS | SSS
- Mobility | Mobility | | Mobility
- Agility | Agility | Agility | Agility
- Speed | Speed | Speed | Speed
- Power | Power | Power | Power
- Strength | Strength | Strength | Strength
- Hypertrophy | Hypertrophy | Hypertrophy | Hypertrophy
- Endurance & MC | Endurance & MC | Endurance & MC | Endurance & MC

TRAINING STRUCTURE: UNSTRUCTURED | LOW STRUCTURE | MODERATE STRUCTURE | HIGH STRUCTURE | VERY HIGH STRUCTURE

YOUTH PHYSICAL DEVELOPMENT (YPD) MODEL FOR FEMALES

CHRONOLOGICAL AGE (YEARS)	2	3	4	5	6	7	8	9	10	11	12	13	14	15	16	17	18	19	20	21+
AGE PERIODS	EARLY CHILDHOOD			MIDDLE CHILDHOOD					ADOLESCENCE									ADULTHOOD	
GROWTH RATE	RAPID GROWTH ↔ STEADY GROWTH ↔ ADOLESCENT SPURT ↔ DECLINE IN GROWTH RATE																				
MATURATIONAL STATUS	YEARS PRE-PHV ← PHV → YEARS POST-PHV																				
TRAINING ADAPTATION	PREDOMINANTLY NEURAL (AGE-RELATED) ↔ COMBINATION OF NEURAL AND HORMONAL (MATURITY-RELATED)																				

PHYSICAL QUALITIES:
- FMS | FMS | FMS | FMS
- SSS | SSS | SSS | SSS
- Mobility | Mobility | | Mobility
- Agility | Agility | Agility | Agility
- Speed | Speed | Speed | Speed
- Power | Power | Power | Power
- Strength | Strength | Strength | Strength
- Hypertrophy | Hypertrophy | Hypertrophy | Hypertrophy
- Endurance & MC | Endurance & MC | Endurance & MC | Endurance & MC

TRAINING STRUCTURE: UNSTRUCTURED | LOW STRUCTURE | MODERATE STRUCTURE | HIGH STRUCTURE | VERY HIGH STRUCTURE

Acknowledgement: Diagram reproduced from Lloyd, Rhodri S. PhD, CSCS*D1; Oliver, Jon L. PhD2 The Youth Physical Development Model: A New Approach to Long-Term Athletic Development, Strength and Conditioning Journal: June 2012 — Volume 34 — Issue 3. Wolters Kluwer.

These two diagrams highlight that there are better windows of opportunity at some stages in your child's development than others. For example, at 14 years of age for boys and 12 for girls is an extended period referred to as 'hypertrophy'. In short, this is hormonally a great opportunity for your child to engage in resistance training and the likes of... WAIT! Don't stop reading now with the 'my child's not going to lift any weights!' (You now know better from chapter 10).

Note also though that the diagram doesn't show that you should only train one parameter and really go after it at any single stage. The emphasis is the different windows. We'll now take a look at how you navigate those windows as a sporting parent.

Early-Middle childhood

This is an exciting time in your child's sporting endeavours, particularly up to the ages of 7 and 8 because boys and girls are relatively equal from a physiological perspective until then — aside from the obvious! During this time they are likely to benefit from plenty of 'unstructured play'. Freedom to move and to move often!

Encourage your child to participate and dabble in a variety of sports, even if you didn't play them yourself as a kid. For example, gymnastics, martial arts and the varying ball sports will all encourage your child to move/explore their limbs in different environments (helping to develop coordination). Coordination will play a key role as your child progresses into adolescence.

Your child participating in a variety of sports can also be a great learning experience for you as a parent. It gives you the opportunity to observe not only the various cultures within different sports, but also coaching styles.

Chapter 12   What does development/maturation mean?

Middle childhood

It's towards the back end of this time that girls will start to demonstrate their superiority over boys (shhhh, don't tell the lads at the pub I said that!).

No, seriously. This should be celebrated as it shows how girls can outshine boys.

This is also a fantastic time to also encourage your daughter to play contact sport! I know, strange concept you might think — bullsh*%t I say! Get amongst it. In most instances they're relatively equal in terms of size. In some instances, girls are larger than same-age boys.

... and no, I'm not referring to the silverback gorilla who looks like he's swallowed a mac truck! Or perhaps, those parents who conveniently forgot their child's birth certificate and are awaiting a new one soon to be cut out of from the back of a Weet-Bix box.

Moderately structured games/sports participation serves your child well between the ages of 5 and 11 for boys and between 5 and 9 for girls. They develop the ability to understand rules and eventually to listen to the coach's sideline antics.

No, I'm not referring to the white line fever of other parents in the team. I mean actually understanding what the coach is asking (in due course).

Adolescence

You know, that fun time like no other when you knew you were destined to be a parent (cough-cough).

As I mentioned earlier in Part 2, this is the time of peak height velocity (PHV) — the most rapid period of growth in your child's development. Understanding PHV implications will enable you to further support rather than criticise your child. Generally, PHV is likely to occur between the ages of 11 to 13 for girls and 13 to 15 for boys.

Think Box

How to Calculate PHV

The age when PHV occurs can be estimated by calculating the 'maturity offset value'. All you need are the following:

- gender
- date of birth
- date of measurement
- standing height (cm)
- seated height (cm)
- weight (kg).

Visit https://www.scienceforsport.com/peak-height-velocity/ and download the Excel workbook if you'd like to estimate the PHV by calculating the maturity offset value for your child.

However, it's one thing understanding and being able to estimate at what stage in your child's maturation PHV is likely to occur, but what does it actually mean?

… Basically, it's a time when you should support your child getting smoked on the outside and being left looking like they're stuck in mud. Or perhaps being towered over in netball and unable to shoot without it being intercepted by an opposing player looking more like Serena Williams than sweet little Sally from next door.

This is the most challenging time for you as a parent and your child's participation in sport. The 'Bambi' or 'baby giraffe' references so often used are bang on.

If you're at the early end of the spectrum, your child will tower over others and almost look like they should be playing up an age group. The only thing stopping them at any time is that they look like they could trip over their own feet!

On the other end, a collision in contact sport may start to look more like a Cooper Mini colliding with a Mack Truck! Hopefully it isn't your little Johnny or Sally when the crowd goes 'Oooooh!'.

Chapter 12 What does development/maturation mean?

But do you want to know the best part of you understanding this time of your child's development? Saving $$$$$!

This isn't the time to go out and invest in that 'trainer to the stars' so they can get 'bigger' and not look so 'small'. Or alternatively, to run faster because they look like they're ability to run or even simply change direction is as confusing as a coffee order in Newtown, Fitzroy, Fremantle or the Valley.

Arrrrgh, the CEO parent.... Their kid has probably been 'offered' an opportunity to train with this academy or that. Pfffft!

It's during middle childhood that the intricacies of rules and specific playing positions can further be cemented with moderately higher-level structured organisation. Kids' understanding of various sports and their role within each sport is further enhanced.

Explore playing positions during this time... and explore often. Not only will it enhance the skills required within a particular sport, it allows your child to further grasp the rules, their understanding of the game and roles within it.

Late adolescence to adulthood

It's here that the exciting development times lie. Increases in strength, power and endurance all continue to provide a window of opportunity to excel, hence the excitement of sport during this age range.

Sport is faster and played with a shift in overall intensity.

This is the time where the reference to your 'child' may not be so applicable anymore. At a glimpse you often confuse them for an adult, and perhaps they may even begin to show you they have muscles in areas you never knew existed!

Hot tip — this is around the time most CEO parents realise their kid's not that special and their projected forecast may need adjusting. Perhaps they should have done that last financial year?! A realistic option is not being listed as a public company, but rather remaining a sole trader/privately owned. Rather than the next Roger Federer, an overseas college perhaps? But don't ask what division… There will be too much time square dancing.

More time than your morning coffee will take to consume anyway.

This is also the time those 'early maturers' who may well have excelled simply from their physical advantage early on often realise they may not be as skilful as they once were… Or perhaps they were never that skilful anyway.

All the while little Johnny/Sonya chipped away at their craft, and in many instances came off second best for their efforts.

But both are now displaying their full sense of the game, their understanding of it, and through 'natural instinct' they're displaying characteristics others 'never knew they had'.

As a sporting parent you did though — all it took was time and 'trusting the process'.

Aside from the physiological benefits (size, strength and fitness) during this stage of development, this is where you're likely to see your return on investment as a sporting parent. And let's just say your moderate risk portfolio is outshining others (cough-cough) through years of compound growth. These payoffs include your adolescent/young adult's:

- fluid movement quality (a fundamental movement skills dividend).
- enhanced eye for the game (right place/right time).
- quality contact (in contact sports) through a combination of timing, technique and physical maturation.
- speed and agility resulting from early locomotor skills acquired and combined with biological changes.
- ability to last the distance/put in sustained high-intensity efforts through accumulated fitness.
- enjoyment/self-driven passion for a particular sport.

Yeah sure, excitement for sport and your child's time in the game is now awesome! But your biggest accomplishment to date?...

They are independently driven by their own desire to succeed and passion for the game!

Chapter 13
Injuries and what they truly mean

Firstly, injuries are a part of sport. They're bound to happen, and that's just it! The earlier you can accept and acknowledge that fact for what it is, the easier they will be to digest when they come your child's way.

However, as a parent there is one injury component that you may just be able to control. Or at least try and minimise. I'm referring to *overuse* injuries during growth and maturation.

The biggest challenge development coaches like me face with your kids is what we refer to as 'training load'. In other words, the extent of your child's sporting commitments. From training, fixtures, multiple sports combined... you get the drift.

Throw in an incredible growth rate and grocery bill to match and it's enough to stop any first time parents in their tracks! 'What?! Am I feeding an army?!' you might ask.

Warning... many of the terms you're about to read will ring alarm bells

Chapter 13 *Injuries and what they truly mean*

unnecessarily! They include words like disease, stress or others that finish with the dreaded 'itis'. But rest assured — your child doesn't have some incurable, rare disease that they've acquired by participating in sport at your local field, courts or pool.

To put it simply, your child will go through many changes in their development (you know, kind of like your little boy/girl went to bed and woke up looking like an adult!). These changes combined with the various demands of sport (whether it be size of equipment used, locomotor movements such as running or jumping and even skills such as hitting, kicking, or swinging) are likely to increase their chances of injury.

Below are four common injuries you may stumble across throughout your child's sporting journey:

- Osgood-Schlatter's disease (tibial apophysitis)
- Sever's disease (calcaneal apophysitis)
- Stress fractures
- Tennis/Golfer's elbow (lateral/medial epicondylitis).

Osgood-Schlatter's disease

No… rest assured (as I highlighted earlier) that this isn't an infectious/incurable disease. Simply put, it is tenderness below the knee as a result of your child's growth. In some instances you may even eventually feel what appears to be a small lump/hardened aspect there. Osgood-Schlatter's disease predominantly happens between the ages of 10 and 15 (remember the PHV concept from chapter 12).

This type of hurdle (and I say 'hurdle' because Osgood-Schlatter's disease doesn't reflect the severity of many other injuries) is likely to occur if your child participates in sports that involve running (including multi-direction sports) and/or jumping… in other words, a large proportion of sports, so don't stress.

For the most part, management simply involves reducing your child's weekly sporting commitments (preferably allowing a day or two between sessions) until their body structures catch up. In other words, prioritise their commitments — it's that simple… In two to three months or so you won't even be thinking about it! 😊

Chapter 13 Injuries and what they truly mean

Sever's disease

Whoa! 'Are you serious?!', you might be thinking. Back-to-back diseases that my child is likely to get purely by participating in sport? Surely not!

Relax... Similar to Osgood-Schlatter's disease, Sever's disease is also related to your child's rate of growth.

Think of an elastic band. As you pull at it, the more it stretches and the more taut it becomes. That places greater stress at either end. Your child's muscles, tendons and bones are no different. The greater your child's rate of growth, the more their calves become stretched, stressing their Achilles tendon and their heel (the anchor point).

As with Osgood-Schlatter's, an appropriate modification to weekly training schedules is a great start to solve the problem (and easily controllable by you).

Adequate footwear and possibly inserts/orthotics are another avenue to explore to either help reduce symptoms or how long they persist.

Once again, don't stress… in the coming months as your child's tissues catch up with their rate of growth, it'll be back-of-mind type stuff!

Stress fractures

This doesn't translate to your child's bone/s breaking by simply going for a run or bowling a cricket ball (despite use of the word 'fracture')… And no, high school exams or a break-up with their first love won't impose that much 'stress' to your child that an imaginable snap will just happen.

The simplest way to look at stress fractures is this — they occur as a result of an inability to overcome/repair the micro-damage caused by repetitive forces. These repetitive forces are nothing out of the ordinary. It just means their body simply can't keep up with all the changes going on. Those repetitive movements such as running, bowling, serving or rowing can be enough to influence micro-damage.

Usual places that stress fractures can happen include the:

- ribs (for example, the forward and backward movements in repetitive sports such as rowing),
- lower back (spondylolysis) from fast bowling in cricket,
- shins (from running/jumping), or the
- feet.

Stress fractures have a similar solution to Osgood-Schlatter's disease and

Sever's disease — manage your child's weekly sporting commitments to reduce the load!

Tennis/Golfer's elbow

While these two injuries aren't exactly the same (they occur on different sides of the forearm/elbow), both result from a similar cause. Repetitive actions/use such as hitting, swinging or throwing.

In a few instances these injuries can become concerning and result in structural changes to the tendon. Some contributing factors may be a new racquet/club/bat, a heavier ball, different string tension or an alteration in action/technique (like throwing, bowling, serving or swinging).

In all other instances there is a simple solution — better weekly schedule management!

The bottom line

There's no doubt that I'm oversimplifying these injuries for you. You'll certainly be better off visiting your local allied health professional for further confirmation/clarity. It goes without saying that a rehabilitation process or adjustments may be required along the way too!

This chapter is by no means a 'do it yourself' botch job. The aim is simply to empower you as with enough knowledge to know you can play a role as a sporting parent in acknowledging to your child that their world isn't ending if they suffer one of these injuries.

I trust that one theme will resonate with you by the end of this chapter... weekly schedule management.

Think Box

Weekly schedule management

Up until approximately 16 years of age*, the simplest indicator I've found to determine whether your child is committing too much time to sport is this formula.[18]

Total hours of structured sport play per week / Child age (Years) = X

The goal should be to ensure that X ≤1 every time. Give it a go and see how your child/children stack up.

If you've hit your schedule management on the head, sing it loud and proud! I'd love to hear about it. Give it a share for a mention @thesportingparent #trainingload.

*NOTE: There are several factors worth considering that may not be applicable to your child's sport. For example, certain sports where maturation plays a heavy role (such as gymnastics or diving, to name a couple). Also, I say up until 16 years of age because that's when participation in supplementary training (i.e. strength training) may start to trend upwards. This will inherently skew the 'structured' play numbers if included.

Overtraining occurs far too often in youth sport and in particular during the crucial years of development. That's why it's important to vary the sports, encourage time off/free play, and even to adopt complementary training/sports as alternatives.

And remember, injuries are a common occurrence in sport. It's how we as sporting parents respond to them that count. As a sporting parent, you are now educated and empowered to understand how the choices you make for your child/children can help to prevent, reduce or manage injuries.

Lesson from the Field #6
Simon Harries

Simon is a true technician. A master of his craft. Not only does his work history display expertise, his academic credentials are nothing to scoff at!

He is an experienced and successful athletic performance specialist in the elite sports industry. He also has an undergraduate degree in Physical Development, Health and Physical Education Teaching and a PhD in Human Physiology.

Simon has extensive experience delivering best-practice outcomes across:

- adolescent strength and conditioning
- long-term athlete development
- sports rehabilitation and injury prevention
- sports science delivery.

He has spent the last decade working as a strength and conditioning coach with elite and developing level athletes across AFL, the NRL and Rugby Australia. During his career he has focused on developing and implementing safe and effective strength and conditioning programs to enable both adolescent and adult athletes to achieve their potential. Recently he has directed his passions towards helping injured athletes to rehabilitate from injury and successfully return to sport.

Simon has also published a number of academic papers across a range of strength and conditioning and sports science disciplines.

You've been one of the very few coaches to have experienced several codes throughout your career, including exposure from the development pathways through to the professional ranks. What do you consider to be the biggest challenge for our youth of today participating in sport?

There are a number of challenges and the evidence is quite clear — youth are more inactive than ever. Cardiorespiratory fitness (or aerobic fitness) and muscular strength levels have declined. Competence in fundamental movement skills (the ability to run, jump, throw, catch and so on) have also declined.

The result is that youth are more underprepared than ever to successfully participate in sport. Reduced levels of fitness and fundamental skills make sport skills more difficult to attain, possibly increase injury risk and make the whole experience less enjoyable. All of those factors ultimately lead to higher drop out rates.

A large portion of your time in recent years has been spent with athlete rehabilitation. Are there any common pitfalls that athletes make in their journey, irrespective of their sport?

A major pitfall is when 'talented' athletes specialise in one sport too early, and then combine that with excessive training loads. These talented athletes experience ever increasing demands to participate in multiple teams and pressure to attend all training sessions. This may predispose them to particular injuries during the rapid periods of growth associated with adolescence. Chronic overuse injuries account for 40-50% of all injuries. Youth athletes who are highly specialised in one sport are 81% more likely to sustain an injury than athletes who are less specialised.[19]

Before specialising in one sport both athletes and their parents need to be well informed about whether early specialisation has been proven to result in enhanced outcomes in adulthood (i.e. a greater chance of playing higher representative levels). And for those that have decided to specialise, there needs to be more open communication between the administrators and coaches of these different teams and the athletes and their parents to strike the right workload balance.

The second mistake youth athletes make is not seeking the right support after injury. Not involving the appropriate specialists often results in poorer decision-making when it comes to returning to sport after an injury. Seeking the advice of qualified specialists will improve the outcome of any rehabilitation and minimise any long-term disruption to physical activity and sport participation.

Given your experience working with the development pathway, what three recommendations would you make to ensure every individual athlete sets themselves up for success in their sporting journey?

1. Play for fun.
Find environments where the youth receives a thoroughly enjoyable and supported physical and social experience. Developing a strong social connection through sport participation can lead to greater chances of maintaining physical activity levels into later adolescence and adulthood.

2. Sample a variety of sports to develop the fundamental skills needed to be a successful mover.
When youth have greater confidence in their ability to perform a variety of

movement skills, they are more likely to participate in sport and persevere in challenging environments.

3. Pursue your passions.
The difference between an athlete who works towards their own goals in a sport they truly enjoy compared to the athlete trying to meet the expectations of others is immense. Once an athlete knows what they love, they can use those internal motivations to set themselves on their sporting journey.

With a background in the educational setting as a qualified teacher and your experience in sport, have you any recommendations for sporting parents to ensure they not only set their kids up for success in sport, but in life?

It's important for you to inform yourselves on the potential avenues for participation and pathway progressions within your child's sport. Having that understanding can alleviate some of the unknown and free you up to focus on your primary role of providing positive support and encouragement for your kids to participate in sport.

If your child does happen to experience an injury, don't be afraid to do your research to find the most appropriate specialists to provide advice and guidance on successful rehabilitation. While most things will improve over time, the right people can ensure your child safely gets back to what they enjoy doing and at the same time minimise any negative outcomes like being dropped from teams or dropping out of sport entirely.

The last but most important recommendation is to make sure you are not only encouraging but providing the right environment for your child to meet the Australian Physical Activity Guidelines for young people.[20]

- For health benefits, young people aged 13–17 years should accumulate at least 60 minutes of moderate to vigorous intensity physical activity every day.

- Young people's physical activity should include a variety of aerobic activities, including some vigorous intensity activity.

- Young people should engage in activities that strengthen muscle and bone on at least three days per week.

- To achieve additional health benefits, young people should engage in more activity — up to several hours per day.

Meeting these guidelines will not only make it easier for your child to participate in sport, being fitter in adolescence reduces the risk of a range of health-related issues in adulthood.

It's also worth reinforcing that in addition to the wide-ranging health benefits there are also substantial social, emotional and intellectual benefits of physical activity and sport participation.

Part 3

Working Towards a Brighter Future

Chapter 14
Building resilient youth

In chapter 5 we delved into 'this generation' and the role you as a sporting parent have played in it. If your score in the parental test (white line fever checklist) wasn't a rude awakening — good. If it was and made you self-reflect… Great!

Either way, empowered with insights that have got you to this part of the book, you should now have an increased awareness of the positive role you can play in your child's sporting development.

That's exactly what your journey as a sporting parent is about. Forever striving for success just as you would expect from your child. Remember, as I highlighted at the start of the book, what's wrong with striving for the best for your child? So, here's to you for persevering as a sporting parent. 😊

Specific parental actions that have failed a generation were outlined in Part 1. Part 2 highlighted the foundations you need to understand to positively influence your child's sporting development. Part 3 is all about how we can create a brighter, more resilient future for your child through their sporting journey.

Let's do this together!

First, let's look at a common issue that you should try and avoid if you want your child to develop resilience — helicopter parenting. This is where you constantly hover over all aspects of your child's life like a helicopter. Below are several ways that helicopter parenting can limit your child's success, but more importantly, how you can avoid it so both you and your child 'win'.

Social skills

As adults, we all experience moments or periods of self-doubt and increased anxiety. Some more so than others. Take a moment to think of a time that was a new experience for you — whether it was a social gathering, meeting a new client or perhaps the first date with your partner in crime who helped you bring your little cherub into this world! I know — goosebumps right?!

Entering a new team is no different for your child. It is daunting for anyone. But it's crucial for developing social skills and building new relationships. By limiting your child's exposure to social opportunities via a single sport and structured training environments, you also limit your child's ability to develop social skills. Not only are social skills essential in sport, they will also help your child in life!

Chapter 14   Building resilient youth

Unstructured play across multiple sports has numerous benefits, including:

- increasing your child's exposure to winning and losing.
- providing an opportunity to create a social pecking order.
- encouraging self-regulation through umpired/refereed games.

All of these benefits can occur without parental influence.

Unstructured play should be encouraged in a safe environment. How youth play in this environment in the absence of (even well-intentioned) adult supervision is very different and we need more of it.

Why not encourage play dates and sport sampling at every opportunity throughout your child's journey? The freedom and ownership that arises from these opportunities is priceless (or free, depending on which way you look at it) and better yet, they build your child's independence.

Game understanding

Specific playing positions may be on that CEO parent's agenda... But not on yours. The truth is that in the majority of team sport instances, there is little to no way of predicting exactly which position your child is likely to be successful at until the maturation process is near complete.

I know — shock factor, right?

If you haven't ever been dropped or played out of your desired position, you simply haven't played sport. So why do parents try to prevent it in far too many instances? Behaviour like that also limits your child's ability to adapt and understand their sport.

There are many benefits that come with not only being dropped but being played out of your desired position too. Let's start first with character. While positive psychology is all the rage in the education system (and with the research/good merit to support it), quite simply it's not always applicable to all facets of life. Sport is a great example of where often it's not.

Understanding what it takes to overcome adversity, try harder and/or learn from your mistakes is essentially a recipe for success in life. Sport is no different.

There are timeless historical examples of athletes who have achieved greatness in their sport while overcoming adversity. Not making a team, being dropped, failing to meet traditional talent ID confinements, or even not being first choice in their preferred playing position are examples of adversity that your child can learn to overcome.

Some adverse things need to be experienced to invoke an emotional response. This response can further build not only your child's passion, but their character too. Encourage your child to develop a mindset that life isn't just all about being on their terms.

You'll often hear that the ability to anticipate what's coming next is what separates great performers from average ones. They can adapt and pivot. Not only will playing out of position increase your child's knowledge of the rules of their sport, it will also enhance their game awareness. The greater variance in exposures across all aspects of a sport will increase their ability to read/anticipate opposition players' moves and space.

So, the next time your child is dropped or played out of position, embrace it. Let your actions and encouraging words as a sporting parent set your child up for success in life. Don't hinder it!

Respect

If you were like me as a child growing up in sport, your parents always instilled that 'you don't get a say' when it comes to coaches and decisions. As a child you may have disagreed with a coach's decision. You may not have been chosen to play a particular time and that made you uncomfortable. You also may not have chosen a particular team mate to be your ally in specific games, but your coach did.

But all too often today, many parents are quick to jump to their kids' defence with coaching decisions. Yet in the majority of instances, they are happy to accept a teacher's classroom decision. Whether it be a grade, punishment of some sort, or simply an opportunity to learn.

... Remember I did say the 'majority' of instances. 😊

So why is sport any different? Unfortunately for some parents it just is! Remember that white line fever?

Your respect for authority figures should be no different in sport than it is in other aspects of your life. On the work front, outcomes need to be addressed, results accomplished and most importantly, the decisions of your boss or those in senior positions accepted. You may not like or agree with the decisions, but as a professional you do need to accept them.

... And I'm not going to lie, sometimes being a bloke even on the home front I/we simply just have to accept it with our #1's (who are absolutely amazing I might add). 😊

If gaining respect from your child is an important part of your parenting (and by you reading this book, I assume it is), then encouraging respect through your actions supporting others is just as important.

Grit

Angela Duckworth, author of the best-selling book *Grit*[21] defines it as 'a combination of passion and perseverance'.

Let's look at passion first. Passion is self-driven or intrinsically motivated, often stemming from the enjoyment of a task, environment, activity or relationship. Kids need to find out what they enjoy doing to build their passion.

If the number one reason for children quitting a sport is a lack of fun, we're limiting the opportunity for them to truly experience it and to cultivate passion. A lack of 'play' is becoming a prominent issue in youth sport development. Many parents are seemingly filling their child with endless opportunities to 'succeed' (when in fact, that approach can very well do the opposite).

Bearing that in mind, let kids play!

Now let's look at the other ingredient of grit — perseverance. Perseverance comes largely from overcoming adversity. There's a sense of accomplishment to persevere and reap the rewards. Providing opportunities for your child to fail and overcome adversity in sport is important.

This stance contrasts with positive psychology. It may facilitate the first part of discovering their 'passion' but possibly fall short on instilling the 'perseverance' necessary to overcome adversity. If all your child does is win or make any team they want, somewhere down the line this is likely to catch up with them. You and I both know that the 'real world' doesn't work that way. So why would you want to encourage your child to live in a safety bubble? It's guaranteed to burst!

This is exactly why gradeless sport might sound like a brilliant idea, but it's simply not. Well at least not for your child's entire sporting journey anyway.

Now I know there are going to be more than a few parents (and educators) opposed to that notion and who actually support gradeless sport.

I agree that there's nothing wrong with your child having 'fun' playing a particular sport. If gradeless sport during the formative years encourages that, then excellent. It may even provide that window of opportunity for your child to gain the confidence to pursue a sport. For that, it's even better!

I also know that one of the most successful determinants of success in the development pathway is children remaining active for life. We should all be striving for this to be our legacy as sporting parents.

Gradeless sport supports this in some instances. Kids who lack confidence or self-belief in their particular abilities or skills can find their place and participate. This is very common in the private schooling framework where sport is mandatory (if not all-year round then at least a summer or winter season of it).

So, what if your child enjoys a particular sport so much that they decide to pursue it further? (Specifically, in the mid-late schooling years). Do they then try out for a team only to realise maybe they weren't as good as they initially thought they were in the supportive gradeless sport/team/or competition they were participating in?

... If so, the struggle continues.

What about acknowledging that ball sports may not be their strong suit and channelling their focus elsewhere instead? They may just become the country's next young promising rower or endurance athlete. But without experiencing adversity, exploring multiple sports or parental support, the opportunity may be missed!

Once again I ask — why would you as a sporting parent wanting your child to live in a safety bubble?!

As sporting parents, we support defeat. We encourage and cultivate it. We acknowledge a lack of ability. We explore multiple sports. And most importantly, we provide an opportunity for our kids to play. All of these things will help our kids to display their true grit in the real-life experiences they'll eventually face in their adult lives.

Support positively and encourage your child to use their strengths. Harness their ability to learn through an open mindset, knowing that opportunity and longevity come from failure/adversity.

Think Box

Parental behaviours

No sporting parent's journey is exactly the same. I encourage you to investigate your own circumstances. I'd like you to not only self-reflect, but to find your own solution.

Social skills

Include an example of how you may have hindered your child's exposure to social skills.

_____
_____
_____

How are you going to set your child up to 'win' with their own social experience/s?

_____
_____
_____

Game understanding

Has there been an instance where you were quick to jump to your child's defence after being dropped or played out of position?

_____
_____
_____

Provide three examples of how you could communicate the benefits of being dropped /played out of position to your child.

1. _____
2. _____
3. _____

Respect

Has there been an instance where you have encouraged your child to have less respect for their coaches through your actions? Whether it be vocal support of their demand for action or physical support in removing them from a school or even sourcing another team?

_____
_____
_____

How are you going to approach a situation like that in future to ensure your child 'wins'?

_____

_____

Grit

Does your child participate in gradeless sport?   **Yes / No**

If you answered 'Yes', proceed to parts A) and B) below.

If you answered 'No', go to part C).

A) Outline three positive outcomes for your child.

1. _____
2. _____
3. _____

B) Identify three positive outcomes you may seek to acquire for your child in graded sport as a sporting parent, as well as how you can make it happen.

1. _____
2. _____
3. _____

C) Has there been a time when your child has been unsuccessful making a team or getting a playing position?

If so, empowered with the knowledge you've gained in this chapter, what action/s would you take as a sporting parent to ensure it is a positive experience for your child?

_____

_____

_____

Lesson from the Field #7
Reed Mahoney NRL

Reed Mahoney is a professional rugby league player for the Parramatta Eels in the NRL. Originally from Queensland, he relocated to Sydney as a 16-year-old without his family to pursue his dreams of playing in the NRL.

I first met Reed as a part of the Parramatta U/20's team. He immediately stood out. In my time working in the development space, there are two things that have stood the test of time for athletes who transition to the professional ranks:

1. Intrinsic motivation

This is an essential prerequisite. Reed was always the first player ready to start training and without fail he completed additional work ('extras') at the end. He was forever seeking feedback about how to improve from a technical, tactical or physical perspective.

2. Self-belief

Reed's self-belief provided him with the confidence to continue to work independently irrespective of what others thought/or were doing. This self-belief has continued into the NRL. I have been fortunate to watch him continue to evolve. In 2018 he was offered a train/trial contract. This meant he could do pre-season with the NRL squad but there were no guarantees of a place in the team. Watching him perform throughout that pre-season was phenomenal. It led to not only a permanent contract, but a debut, and now a regular starting spot in the Parramatta roster... and his journey continues!

Seeing him go from strength to strength now mixing it up with seasoned first graders is exceptional. Reed epitomises resilience.

As a kid growing up in Australia, what sports did you play?

As a kid I just wanted to play every sport I could, preferably anything with a ball. I played rugby league and cricket the most.

I have two older brothers and we were all doing it together. Rugby league throughout winter and cricket throughout summer.

While my Dad played a bit of footy at a local level when he was young, it was more following in my older brother's footsteps that encouraged me to play.

As I got older and into my teenage years I then got into other sports like OzTag and touch, which was more time spent playing footy.

At what age did you begin to take your rugby league seriously and how did that come about?

I began to take it more seriously from about the age of 15. That included giving up cricket and other alternatives to focus more on my footy. Summer then transitioned into a pre-season for a representative team which took up more time.

When I was 15 I also played in a national schoolboy rugby league championship. That resulted in me getting picked up by the Canterbury Bulldogs. Once that happened it all became a little more serious.

Around the same age I also started doing strength training too! Initially I did all TRX (suspension trainer) stuff on my own. That led to me becoming obsessed with the gym. I enjoyed that type of training as it began with my body weight at first and progressed from there.

Not being a naturally big guy, I also did a little gym work at school and then would venture out doing other stuff after school.

Were you always in the top teams as a kid?

Actually, I wasn't.

The team I started playing in from about 6 to 13 years of age were the Beerwah Bulldogs. We weren't the strongest team and only played in the B-division.

At one stage we got moved up to the A-division but every weekend without fail we were getting flogged 40-50 nil! Unfortunately, we were too good for B-division but not strong enough for A-division.

Turning up and getting pumped every weekend was more than frustrating as a kid!

As I got older, I got over the losses but I knew I was better than B-division. Back then it was all about having fun, although everyone in the team was competitive... we just weren't good enough.

Personally, I wasn't getting any better, but I wasn't getting any worse. At the end of the U/14 season I got a call from the Redcliffe Dolphins. For the next 6 weeks I spent pre-season at the Dolphins in their U/15's summer squad.

It was an hour drive to and from training at Redcliffe which was obviously a big demand on my parents. For them to be working all day, then take me to training while factoring in my other siblings — that's a big ask!

Eventually in time it led me to going to the Kawana Dolphins. Being only 20-25 minutes from home, it was a decision I had to make.

It was difficult leaving mates behind at a young age. But if I wanted to go anywhere with my footy, again it was a decision I had to make.

Have you ever been dropped or played out of position throughout your journey? And if so, what advice did your parents have for you?

I've been fortunate that I was never really dropped from a team. I did get placed in other positions but it was more to see how I would go there.

I've been close to being dropped in the NRL, which is a scary thought. It's just motivated me to go deeper within myself to work on my own game or ability as an individual.

On another note though would be my experience at the Bulldogs with not even making a team.

I was signed to their SG Ball side (U/18s) and was a regular starter all year. Then I got a minor injury and came back off the bench. After several weeks I earned my spot back. I transitioned into the U/20's squad and completed 6 or so weeks there until it got to the time of contracts and resigning.

… It was then that I was told I wasn't going to be picked in the 20's squad for the next two years. They had put money into other players and I was going to be third string!

About a week later I got a call from Parramatta and pretty well came straight over.

My parents have always told me to do what I think is best for me. At Canterbury I was still very young, only 18. They encouraged my decision by asking 'What have you got to lose?'.
I knew when making the shift that I just had to work hard to get what I wanted!

You relocated from Queensland at a relatively young age (turning 17 the year you came down to Sydney). What made you decide to do that? And in the absence of family and friends, it must have been pretty tough. How have you found the experience and do you have any advice for up-and-coming athletes who may one day find themselves in your position?

It was pretty hard! I struggled for about the first year or so. I didn't know anyone, didn't have a car, was on foot all the time, and my parents would only come down whenever they could. As a 17-year-old that's pretty tough!

It wasn't all bad though, the 'Bulldog house' was great! At any one time there were approximately 5 or so of us players who had all relocated and were in the same boat.

The best advice I could give to anyone doing the same thing would be to establish a routine. Once I got a job and knew where I was going, I was set and didn't have too much time to sit around thinking about things.

For me, routine and getting a bit of rhythm certainly helped me cope with the situation. I could focus on my footy without diverting my attention to things I may have been missing out on back home.

The house parents I lived with were always very supportive too!

You were on a train/trial contract going into the 2018 pre-season. What was going through your mind entering into one of the toughest challenges in your career?

I got a phone call about two-and-a-half weeks before pre-season started. I was actually in a meeting at work but I took the call and that was it! For me it was always about a 'head-down, arse-up' mentality! That's what has got me to where I am today.

I've always prided myself on hard work. I never thought I was the most talented player but I could be the most hard-working player... you work hard and you can get what you want!

With football skills and the physical side, I just had to get through it all by working hard.

Obviously though I had back-to-back days in that particular pre-season (being my first) where I struggled. I was training with guys who were a lot bigger than me. Those first 6 weeks were the hardest I've ever trained!

After the first few weeks I started to dip a bit. Mentally and physically it just takes its toll. I knew I had to start preparing myself mentally to get through the week. It's always going to be hard.

I went into every day thinking 'it's going to be hard today!'. I started to find that instead of shying away from it, my mentality shifted to embracing the grind. This led me to a realisation that I was actually going alright — keeping up with everyone with the football skills and the physical.

As a current professional athlete, how would you define success in sport?

That's a tough question.

On an individual level, I think winning premierships. Then there's representative honours. If I can tick those boxes by the time I retire, then I'll be satisfied with everything I've done.

Success is more than an individual though. Playing a team sport it's down to everyone in the squad. If every player in the team achieves one good thing, then I feel it translates to everyone achieving it.

More recently the success of a few players in our team playing State of Origin is the result of the success that we have had as a team. It put them in that position.

In sport I feel like the individual accolades you receive aren't possible without the success of your team-mates.

Chapter 15
Parent/child friendships

On the last day of the school term there's not a kid in the country who doesn't want to get out of there ASAP! If you were like me as a kid growing up, you'd pull every stunt in the book with the 'We don't do anything on the last day anyway!' line to try and get out of even turning up... or to 'kick-start the school holidays early' as some might say.

Education is important and tertiary qualifications are one thing, but there's a reason why most require a 'prac' component. It enables you to gain experience and learn first-hand the things they don't teach you in the textbooks or online these days. (Facepalm — there I go again with 'these days' and starting to sound more and more like my parents).

As a coach, I'm proud to say most of the quality lessons I've learnt haven't come from studying but from tried and tested methods to the madness. None more so than in the educational sector.

Some of the biggest lessons I learnt were at Westfields Sports High School and I'm very grateful. Westfields is a proud, selective sporting school in south-west

Sydney, rich in accomplishments and it has no shortage of talent. In fact, I'd go as far as saying that its talent can't be beat nationwide. Their alumni stretches far and wide both nationally and internationally in the professional sporting arena over decades and across multiple sports.

Successful?... Bloody oath!

But there was a broad spectrum of socio-economic variance in the school population and the home life for some students was let's just say 'better left there'... School was their only escape and in many instances their athletic prowess saved them from a very different youth path.

That last day of school at Westfields was one of the first things that stood out to me. Every term without fail the same students were outside the gym on the last day. Whether it be still trying to get in or just chilling outside while their mates were inside. I'm unsure how many actually went to all their classes on that day each term, but hey if they continued to do right by my expectations and rules within the gym then so be it, I was happy to turn a blind eye... (I never told them that though!)

They were already a step ahead of me anyway as a youth by actually turning up.

This cohort was different. Those I'd expected to be truant on the last day weren't. And those that I least expected to be were. Every term it was the same. Those deemed troublemakers, loose units, rogue offenders or whatever term the educational sector tried to label them with (having been one myself I didn't care much for labels I might add).

They were always there, the last to leave the school grounds!

Why? Because what children/youth crave in relationships is often very different to what we do as adults. Discipline, understanding, respect, expectations and repercussions were all an integrative aspect of the relationships I had with these students.

Sure, 'run ins' (if you want to call them that) occurred, I'm not going to lie. But I'd prefer to refer to them as 'testing the boundaries', 'seeking attention' or 'discipline' incidents, depending on which side of the fence you're looking at them from.

These young 'offenders' were always there because they craved their friendships, routine and expectations. They either didn't get those things at home, or they got very little. In some instances, they were 'starved'!

While I might have entered the Westfields' school grounds every last day with an ambitious list of tasks to accomplish before the final bell to be ready for day one of the next school term, they were never accomplished. Looking back (with very fond memories), I'm glad they weren't. I learnt a very valuable lesson instead. It taught me not only the importance of relationships and the need to bond as humans, but exactly why you can't be 'friends' with a child when you're in a position of authority. As a parent, this lesson is very relevant to you.

You hear it all the time, and if you haven't heard it at least once maybe you will in the near future — 'My son/daughter is my best friend!'.

Am I the only one who thinks it weird that someone might want their 7 or 10-year-old to be their best friend?! In fact I'd go as far as to say that if you saw your friend hanging at a bus stop with a child of that age and referring to them as their 'best friend', you'd be concerned and might even feel the need to possibly make a phone call.

As a sporting parent, it's crucial for you to have boundaries with your child/children. These boundaries will not only enhance your relationship, but also increase their likelihood of sporting success. We all want the best for our children. You wouldn't be reading this book otherwise. Why should you shy away from that? You shouldn't, so let's bloody celebrate it!

'Give me one good reason why I shouldn't be my child's best friend', you might be thinking. Sure, I'll give you a few:

- Children are intuitive (and at times, manipulative).

    Regardless how young they are, they will use things to their advantage. Remember back to when little Joey/Alicia were bubs? If they cried loud enough, they knew they could get a feed or some attention before bed. Fast forward a couple of weeks/months and they may have cried earlier and earlier depending on how their wants (as opposed to their needs) were met by your previous responses.

    This intuition only increases the older they get, as do their wants from you as a parent. Remember, your kids are children and you are an adult.

- There are invaluable lessons to be learnt from sport that are very applicable to life.

    Many of these lessons are outcomes of being placed in situations your child may not 'choose' to be in. Yet they are character building. The greatest impact of many of these lessons is in them being experienced by your child rather than in them being told. Expose them to these lessons. In due course, any brief moments of pain will be forgotten but the lesson will have been learnt and life-lasting character traits acquired along the way.

- Emotional connections can be influential in the decision-making process.

    But here's the thing. If you place your 'best friend' hat on with your child, that can be precisely what prevents many valuable lessons from being learnt. You'll want to protect, remove and seek a more positive experience for them. In contrast, when you have your parent hat on, those same situations can be deemed as invaluable character-building lessons for your child. Understand the difference? One perspective is defensive, the other is embracive. Both have an emotional connection and drive, but each seeks different outcomes. Be embracive!

By the way, can you guess which Westfields' students were the ones to ask the first 'why' question when being informed of my decision to move on to another employer? Which students were welling up when trying to understand why?

Yep you guessed it. Those same ones who turned up every last day of the school term. They actually made me second guess myself as I sat in the carpark leaving for the last time. I'd be lying if I didn't say it made me feel 'tight in the chest' (in my most masculine voice).

But it just proves the importance of relationships and boundaries. Lines in the sand, expectations or any other term you'd like to place on this concept. Boundaries which being your child's best friend won't permit!

Chapter 16
Framing

Communicating with your kids is certainly one of the most challenging aspects of being a parent. It can be a 24-hour job! And your little Gremlins (loveable of course) are always listening or watching your every move!

Throw in the passion of sport and the emotions/white line fever of your child's teammate's parents (because as a sporting parent you would never do that 😊)… communication is certainly influential.

So, let me introduce you to a communication concept you may not have thought much about … or even heard of for that matter — framing!

Framing is simply choosing a word that is likely to positively alter your perception of an experience. To give this concept some context, I'll give you an example of what I faced as a coach several years ago. It might strike a chord.

On this particular day, a parent (let's call him Alberto) cold-called me to discuss his child's (let's call him Dillon) commitment (or lack of it) to his 'recovery rides'. An avid cyclist was Alberto (no, cycling wasn't part of the school's sporting options) ... oh, and Dillon. Alberto was enquiring if there was any 'research' into the optimal kilometres children should be riding per week? (Remember that emotional attachment to sporting selection? Like father, like son).

CEO parent?... You think?!

Firstly, I'll point out I'm not from a cycling background, but secondly, I'm pretty confident there isn't an idealistic number to answer his question for a 12-year-old boy (Year 7), let alone one supported by research.

As the conversation evolved, it turned out Dillon would accompany Alberto and his cycling buddies on their weekly recovery rides. Alberto was concerned that Dillon wasn't as passionate about the recovery rides as he was. Instead, he was more in tune/aligned with Alberto's mate's distaste for them.

... enter the concept of framing. I queried how Dillon knew they were 'recovery rides' and how Alberto had decided to structure these into Dillon's weekly training schedule... or financial forecast? (Whoops — yes, I did just write that part!)

Alberto had referred to the rides as 'recovery rides', as would his cycling buddies. So, after acknowledging my lack of a detailed understanding of the sport and what the true definition of a 'MAMIL' actually meant (Middle Aged Men in Lycra), I introduced the framing concept and asked if any thought had been given to it.

Aside from suggesting a possible ditch of the recovery rides (remembering Dillon was still playing sport for his school which further contributed to his excessive weekly training loads), I suggested reframing these recovery rides.

Side note — ditch the recovery ride due to excessive training loads?! Was I mad? Yep totally, to a CEO parent, I can be M-A-D!

Dillon only knew of them as recovery rides due to being informed that's what they were by Alberto. He then had a choice to conform and enjoy them like his father, or rebel and possibly get some additional reinforcement (otherwise known as 'likes' these days) from the road gang by further supporting their suggestive comments.

Chapter 16 Framing

He had chosen option B, which for him might have felt great getting a few back slaps from the lads! It was probably one of the reasons for Alberto's call.

I suggested the rides be referred to as 'technical sessions' moving forward. That way Dillon no longer looked at the negative connotation of recovery rides, but rather at an additional opportunity to work on his technique and possibly build a further bond with his father through positive reinforcement. This framing was a revelation to Alberto!

I also told Alberto to tip the rest of the gang off on what he and Dillon would be working on so that Dillon could enjoy the moment more and possibly get further positive reinforcement from the other gents in floral Lycra. Gamechanger!

Alberto contacted me a few weeks later to say what a great idea it was. Not only had Dillon really progressed, but he was stoked they had ditched the recovery rides to give him extra time to work on his technique.

To me it highlighted one thing for parents. You have the maturity, life experience and foresight to shape your child's perception of the world and their experiences within it. Choose your language wisely and try framing to get the best out of your child in situations like Alberto was facing.

But there's only a small window of opportunity where framing can work a treat before kids realise you're trying to pull the wool over their eyes. Embrace that window! Because when it closes, you'll realise that your child (or by that stage independent teenager) may have an opinion. In some instances, they may not even want to go for rides with you and your crew anymore, preferring to start a crew of their own instead!

Think Box

Has there been an instance where your child (<12 years of age) may have potentially agreed with a biased opinion you had about their situation?   Yes / No

- If you answered 'Yes', what was the situation?

_____
_____
_____

- If you answered 'No', can you think of an example situation where your child would?

_____
_____
_____

What steps/parties would also be necessary to ensure your framing was a success? And how would you negotiate the support of any other parties?

Chapter 17
What do you truly want for your child? (Professional sport vs active for life)

Success and the definition of it will vary between sporting parents. You may or may not have thought of your definition during your child's journey yet.

Whether you've only just started or are about to release your lovable hounds (otherwise known as young adults) into the world, it's something to think about.

Take a moment to pause and reflect.

What exactly is it you hope/d to obtain from your child's sporting endeavours? Did you start out on those frosty Saturday mornings dreaming of your child playing professional sport? Or like most Aussie families, was playing sport simply a means to encourage your kids to be active for life and make healthier life-long choices?... Or most importantly, just to have fun and be happy?

Chapter 17   What do you truly want for your child? (Professional sport vs active for life)

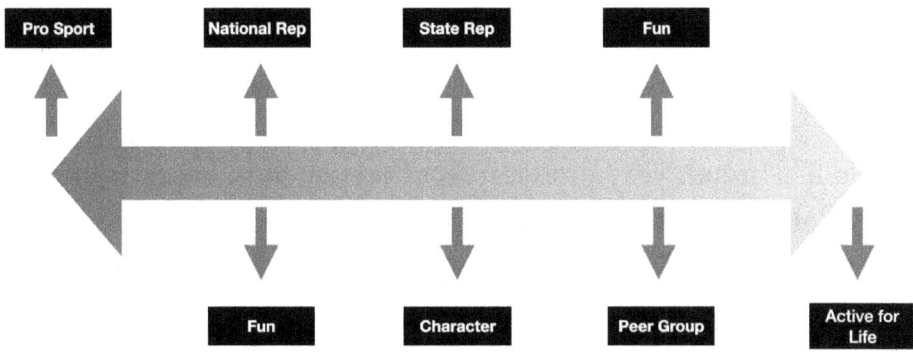

Image 2. Youth sport participation continuum

In many instances, your perception of your child's sporting pathway may also vary along the way. Having dabbled in 'multiple sports' like any good sporting parent should encourage, you and your child may have experienced some early success. Whether being selected for a local, state, or national representative team or simply developing a quality friendship circle, your child is reaping the benefits as a maturing individual.

Early success and other participating parents may encourage you to think even deeper about the evolving path you as a family are going to take.

Professional sport

As I mentioned in chapter 9, the likelihood of your child playing professional sport is very low. By no means am I trying to shatter your dreams if this is what your definition of success for your child/children is.

But props to you as a sporting parent should your child be one of the few to have reached that level! No doubt your sacrifices have been countless. Financial, career, time, relationships and personal desires have all amounted to your child's opportunity in whatever sport. With any luck and plenty of hard work, season upon season they'll make a career out of it, largely because of your sacrifices.

You should feel proud. Very proud in fact that you have not only produced a quality athlete with the ability to turn their passion into a career, but also one who is a role model for many aspiring kids around the country. It takes not only an incredible amount of dedication from a parenting perspective, but commitment both physically and mentally from your child.

Active for life

The unfortunate reality is that national physical activity is on the decline among our youth. As I highlighted in chapter 3, technology advances are not only making our lives easier, but also encouraging less physical activity.
It's predicted that 81% of youth between the ages of 11 and 17 are insufficiently physically active around the globe![22] Within Australia the figure is 71%. That's nearly 3 in every 4 children![23] We are facing an uphill battle to ensure the future generations are adequately physically prepared not only for sport but for life!

But as I highlighted in chapter 1, every week in Australia 3.2 million take the field, court, hall or whatever their opportunity of choice is to be active. This sheer number alone indicates the important role sport can play in getting our youth more physically active.

If you ask sporting parents whose children have made it in the professional ranks why they got their kids into sport in the first place, many will say 'I just wanted them to have fun'. (A surprise to some of you? It's true!).

Chapter 17   What do you truly want for your child? (Professional sport vs active for life)

Irrespective of where we as sporting parents envisage our kids ending up, that fun factor will not only determine their level of commitment in playing sport, but also their adherence to it.

Did you know that kids with physically active parents are more likely to be active themselves? 72% of children who have at least one active parent are physically active in organised sport or physical activity outside of school[24]... Well now you do!

But as a parent it's not only about your participation in physical activity or sport. Being actively involved in various facets of sport is even better! Nearly 90% of kids with at least one parent who not only plays but volunteers in sport are active in organised sport or physical activity outside of school!

If you've made it this far in the book, you'll acknowledge the impact of sport and the many lessons it teaches our kids. Unquestionably it plays an important role in setting them up for life. Your success as a sporting parent can only be judged by you alone and your interpretation of what that success looks like. Now that you understand how we've failed a generation and you know the ingredients required to build the foundations for your child's sporting journey, how are you going to define success of their participation?

Think Box

What sports would I like my child to play?
_____
_____
_____
_____

Do I have an emotional connection to any of these sports as a parent? If so, what is it and how did it come about?
_____
_____
_____
_____

Having read the previous chapters in this book, are there any new sports I might consider encouraging my child/children to sample? If so, what are they and how have my thoughts changed?
_____
_____
_____
_____

Chapter 17   What do you truly want for your child? (Professional sport vs active for life)

How would I define sporting success for my child?
_____
_____
_____

Finish this sentence: 'When it's all said and done as a sporting parent, I can only hope for my child (insert name here_____) to be:
_____
_____
_____
_____

as a result of the decisions I've made and the actions I've displayed in their sporting journey!

We'd love to hear your success story. Give it a share — tag @thesportingparent and #ourjourney

Chapter 18
Sport and the lessons of life

You've made it! Massive props to you as a sporting parent!

It's been one hell of a ride.

I've no doubt you've enjoyed and at times even protested against some of the concepts within this book. Great! Celebrate all aspects of becoming a better sporting parent and individual along the way.

Knowledge is key, regardless of where you are on your journey as a sporting parent. By sticking it out, digesting the information presented, participating in the 'Think Boxes' and taking the time to value the 'Lessons from the Field', you're now empowered to make better decisions. Decisions that are likely to give you the confidence to move forward, stumble, fall and rise again to continue to accomplish your definition of sporting success for your child/children.

At the end of the day, no one ever said being a parent was going to be easy... and being a sporting parent, well……

Rest assured, the following lessons in life can be attributed to the sporting journey you're on with your kids and as a family. They're in safe hands. Your hands.

Resilience

Chapter 14 detailed how to build resilience in our youth. No matter where you currently are as a sporting parent in your journey, rest assured the resilience your child is building through sport will continue well beyond the sporting arena into adulthood. The countless opportunities you've experienced along the way will all be worth it. Yes, I refer to them as 'opportunities' no matter how frustrated you currently are or have been in the past.

Every loss, failure to make a team, time played out of position and possible disagreement with a coach's decision... they're all worth it. Sport teaches your child valuable lessons. Embrace the opportunity sport provides to help your child become resilient!

For every hurdle your grown child faces in life (like a missed job opportunity, the end of a childhood sweetheart relationship, outgrowing childhood peer groups or challenging their sexuality) the resilience acquired through sport will place them in better stead. They will see these challenges as opportunities to not only survive, but to prosper.

Teamwork

Irrespective of whether your kids are currently playing, have played or you're planning on them playing a team-based sport, teamwork is essential across the board in the sporting arena. This includes parents as well as kids.

Your teamwork contribution as a sporting parent might be driving another child to a weekly sporting fixture to help out and ensure they make it. It may be baking the cakes, manning the barbecue or selling tickets in your local club's raffle.

The best part of all that?... Through your positive contribution as a sporting parent leading through your actions, you'll contribute to your child's attitude towards jumping in and having a go to support others.

Playing a team sport reinforces to your kids that the world isn't only about them. Others need an opportunity to play, receive a pass, score a try, or even borrow some kit when they've forgotten their own as scatterbrain teenagers.

Teamwork is crucial in the wider world beyond sport for the success of your child as an individual, within an organisation, or eventually even with their prospective partner and becoming a sporting parent.

By you encouraging their participation in sport, they will have learnt through experience that teamwork will not only help them as individuals to flourish, but others too!

Independence

A crucial part of raising kids is encouraging their independence. Through your direct parenting and their participation in sport, our youth of today will be better equipped to make decisions. Not only making them, but being accountable for them!

Even from the early days, encourage them to remember their boots, pack their kit bag, or at least provide the correct weekend fixture information to you (the 'unofficial' Uber driver).

There's also the discipline of selecting a sport, adhering to it and seeing it through until the end of the season regardless of their experiences (both positive or negative) along the way.

Both team and individual sports encourage independence and accountability. Kids simply couldn't participate throughout their entire youth without experiencing some form of independence.

Embrace it!... And do it early on in your journey as a sporting parent. Every independent step along the way helps to ensure that our youth of today become confident and accountable decision-makers to succeed not only in sport, but to navigate their way through life!

Respect

In chapter 14 we delved into what it meant for both you as a parent and your child to display respect through your actions.

Helicopter parenting becomes problematic when our youth of today have a 'get-out clause'. If they do and they're on the rough end of the stick so to speak from a coach's decision, it's easy to fall back into default mode. That mode may well be the attitude of 'I'll just get my parents to sort it!'.

On more than one occasion I personally (and countless teachers around the country) have been faced with an irate parent on the end of the phone jumping to the defence of their little cherub.

Unfortunately, in most instances these defences haven't been briefed with the correct facts or the full side of the story. Well-meaning parents are trying to look out for their child's best interest, but in fact are offering them (or supporting) their 'get out clause'.

This becomes more problematic in the big bad world when these kids grow up. They become disruptive, defensive, answering back or simply ignoring requests from their superiors because they have been raised with the 'this doesn't apply to me' mentality.

At the completion of your journey as sporting parents, not only will your kids be OK with following orders, they will also respect them as a part of their place in the world. A world that would involve their positive contribution to it as opposed to avoidance.

Values

Values vary from individual to individual. They may also vary from sport to sport. However, there are some common values among sports. Ones that ensure individuals contribute positively to society. Ones that hold strong under duress. Values play a strong part in kids' upbringing. Participation in sport will reinforce and instil values in your child via the teams they're a part of, the friendship circles embraced and the culture of sports participated in (i.e. whether individual or team-based)

Irrespective of where your child ends up (firstly as a young adult and eventually in adulthood), how these values stand the test of time will be heavily determined by the extent that you as a sporting parent have nurtured and led by example.

Kudos to you — the sporting parent and the endless time you invest throughout their journey. Countless financial sacrifices to ensure they not only participate but are actively engaged in various sporting endeavours. These values may well be the legacy you as a sporting parent leave behind via your child's future contribution to the world!

Lesson from the Field #8 – Chloe Dalton

Chloe is one of Australia's very few elite, triple sport athletes. After playing basketball in the WNBL with the Sydney Uni Flames, she transitioned to rugby. She debuted for the Australian Rugby Sevens' team in 2014, winning gold at the 2016 Rio Olympics. Chloe was recognised as Australia's top player in 2017, winning the Shawn Mackay Medal.

Not long afterwards she crossed codes, making her debut for Carlton in the AFLW in 2019 and playing in a grand final in front of 53,000 in her first season. She was the runner-up in Carlton's Best and Fairest Awards in 2020 and is currently training with the Aussie Sevens' team in Sydney in preparation for the postponed Tokyo Olympics in 2021.

Chloe is also an Order of Australia Medal recipient for Service to Sport and she graduated from the University of Sydney in 2017 with a Bachelor of Applied Science (Physiotherapy). She has particular interest in neurological physiotherapy, supporting those affected by stroke, Parkinson's Disease and brain injuries.

Recently Chloe created *The Female Athlete Project* podcast, sharing much needed insights into female journeys in elite sport from world champions, fellow Olympians and others at the top of their game!

You've reached the pinnacle for many athletes around the world... an Olympic gold medal, as well playing professionally at the highest level in three different sports. What are the three biggest lessons sport has taught you?

1. Change can be daunting, but it allows you to grow in multiple areas of your life. I remember instances of feeling overwhelmed and out of my depth, and I often questioned whether I'd made the right decision in changing sports. Not long after I started playing rugby, I read a quote from Steve Jobs that really resonated with me — "The heaviness of being successful was replaced by the lightness of being a beginner again."

    I think there is a real sense of freedom that comes with allowing yourself to be okay with not having all the answers. It enables you to feel comfortable asking questions, seeking feedback and acting with humility when you approach different tasks. I believe there is no limit on how much you can achieve when you approach a challenge with a teachable mindset.

2. "There's more in you than what you think you've got." This is a mantra I often say to myself when I feel like I have nothing left to give — whether in the final repetition of a gruelling conditioning set, during a hard gym session at the end of a long week of training or in the dying minutes of a game. I feel incredibly grateful for the way sport has taught me to be resilient, to push through in those moments when I felt like giving up. Sport has taught me that there is always more in me than I think I've got left.

3. You don't have to fit into a specific box to be successful. Growing up I often thought that I had to be the perfect athlete to achieve my goals. I think the longer

I've played sport, the more I've realised that I perform at my best when I do what works best for me. That often takes a lot of trial and error over time, but I think the important message is that kids don't have to put pressure on themselves to fit a specific mould. The most successful teams I've played with have had a really diverse mix of personalities, backgrounds, strengths and weaknesses.

What has been your biggest challenge in your career, and what strategies did you use to overcome it?

The biggest challenge in my career so far was when I fractured my left arm three times in the space of 12 months in the lead up to the Rio Olympics. During that 12 months I had multiple surgeries — artificial bone inserts, bone grafts from my hip, and plates and screws inserted along the length of my forearm (which I still have in there today).

I vividly remember sitting in the surgeon's office after fracturing my arm for the third time. I was studying to become a physiotherapist, and the surgeon said to me that I really needed to consider whether continuing to play rugby was going to put my future physio career at risk.

Mum and I went outside and sat on the park bench, both in tears. It was less than nine months out from a chance to represent my country at an Olympic Games. I said to Mum, "I've wanted to win an Olympic gold medal since I was seven years old, I'm not going to stop playing now."

After the final surgery, I was really limited in terms of the training I could do with only one arm. I decided to use the time as an opportunity to work on my dropkicking. I wanted to become the best dropkicker in the World Series. I spent hours working on my kicking technique, restarts and conversions. When I made my comeback the following season, I was the leading goal kicker in the 2016 World Series.

What sports did you play as a kid growing up in Australia? And how were they usually chosen? (i.e. Parental influence from what they played, or did you select them and they supported you?)

I played a whole range of sports growing up — soccer, baseball, athletics, touch footy, cross country, nippers and basketball. I think that athletics and cross country had some parental influence as my Mum and her Dad were both great runners growing up.

I only ever played sports that I enjoyed and wanted to play, and if I decided I wanted to try something new, Mum and Dad were incredibly supportive. Looking back, it's insane to think about the amount of hours that they devoted to my sport, whether driving me around, standing on the sidelines cheering or giving up long weekends for tournaments.

When we won gold in Rio, the first thing I did after embracing my teammates was run towards the crowd. I was lifted up into the stands by my immediate and extended family. I felt an overwhelming sense of gratitude for everything they had contributed to my sporting journey over many years, and I couldn't have asked for anything more than to have them there for that moment.

You're now training and playing with others in your team who were young enough to watch you and your teammates compete and win gold in the Rio Olympics. That must be special. To the young athletes watching and aspiring to be in your shoes one day — what would be your biggest advice to them?

My biggest piece of advice to young athletes would be to choose to do whatever you enjoy, and not make decisions based on other people's opinions.

When I was changing codes to AFLW, there were a few people who made remarks like, 'Oh, you're changing sports again'. At the time I didn't know how to respond, and it made me doubt whether it showed a lack of commitment on my behalf.

I decided to embrace the criticism, because at the end of the day, I was choosing to do what I wanted to do to challenge myself and learn new things. I have met so many incredible people along my sporting journey and I wouldn't change a single part of it.

What is your definition of success in sport for anyone who participates in it?

My definition of success in sport is to finish the season as a better player than you were before. I think this applies in a physical sense — getting faster, fitter, stronger and more skilled. But more importantly for me, it's learning new things about yourself, putting yourself in situations that challenge you, becoming more empathetic, building new relationships and having a good time.

Conclusion

There are no greater challenges in life than being a parent, especially a sporting parent.

Sporting parents are selfless, passionate, fearless, and above all, they want the best for their kids. As I highlighted as the start of the book, that's nothing to be ashamed about.

If you're not trying your best for your kids by supporting them and their pursuits regardless of what they are in life, then what are you doing as a parent?

For me, this book had to be done. I want to help all Australian sporting parents and families to achieve whatever their definition of success is. Each of you are on your own journey.

If there were elements of this book you loved — awesome! If you disagreed with some (or even became outright frustrated), good on you for persevering and getting to where you are now.

One thing's for certain though, I have no doubt you have taken something from this book. You're now educated and empowered to make enhanced judgements to help you succeed in your journey.

This book couldn't have come to fruition if it wasn't for the amazing contributors. Whether sharing their personal experiences or professional knowledge and opinions, their contributions certainly added greater depth and supported a well-rounded approach, rather than you just reading my opinions.

Every one of them agreed to contribute and never once asked for anything in return… That's what makes passionate people building a positive future great!

If there's one resource I hope every local sports club, coach, teacher, health professional and parent can lean on as a reference… I hope it's this book!

Australia is a proud sporting nation. We love an underdog, and we love even more for our world to stop and to watch our greatest athletes perform on the biggest stage in their events. There are too many great Australian sporting icons to name here who have captivated everyone in the country with their *moment of greatness*.

This book is written for Australians. Bloody oath! It didn't make sense to me to produce a general, global book. We as Aussies do it like no other — and for that I'm grateful. I've loved every minute of sharing my thoughts with you and contributing to building the generations to come.

I encourage you to share your journey with me @thesportingparent on all social media platforms. I'd love to see you applying the principles in this book and watch you and your family evolve through all your triumphs and tribulations!

Endnotes

1. Australian Sports Commission, 2016. *AusPlay: Participation data for the sport sector.*
2. Faigenbaum, A.D., Rebullido, T.R., Peña, J. et al. *Resistance Exercise for the Prevention and Treatment of Pediatric Dynapenia.* J. of SCI. IN SPORT AND EXERCISE 1, 208–216 (2019). https://doi.org/10.1007/s42978-019-00038
3. Faigenbaum AD, MacDonald JP, Stracciolini A, Rebullido TR. *Making a Strong Case for Prioritizing Muscular Fitness in Youth Physical Activity Guidelines.* Curr Sports Med Rep. 2020 Dec;19(12):530-536. doi: 10.1249/JSR.0000000000000784. PMID: 33306516
4. Schneuer, F.J., Bell, J.C., Adams, S.E. et al. *The burden of hospitalized sports-related injuries in children: an Australian population-based study, 2005–2013.* Inj. Epidemiol. 5, 45 (2018). https://doi.org/10.1186/s40621-018-0175-6
5. Shaw, L.; Finch, C.F. *Trends in Pediatric and Adolescent Anterior Cruciate Ligament Injuries in Victoria, Australia 2005–2015.* Int. J. Environ. Res. Public Health 2017, 14, 599
6. https://app.education.nsw.gov.au/sport/File/4344
7. https://www.sportaus.gov.au/media_centre/news/sport-australia-releases-position-statement-on-physical-literacy-to-support-our-nations-health/_nocache
8. Collins, H., Booth, J.N., Duncan, A. et al. *The effect of resistance training interventions on fundamental movement skills in youth: a meta-analysis.* Sports Med — Open 5, 17 (2019). https://doi.org/10.1186/s40798-019-0188-x
9. Jaakkola T, Yli-Piipari S, Huotari P, Watt A, Liukkonen J. *Fundamental movement skills and physical fitness as predictors of physical activity: A 6-year follow-up study.* Scand J Med Sci Sports. 2016 Jan;26(1):74-81. doi: 10.1111/sms.12407. Epub 2015 Feb 2. PMID: 25644386

10 Hardy LL, Barnett L, Espinel P, Okely AD. Thirteen-year trends in child and adolescent fundamental movement skills: 1997-2010. Med Sci Sports Exerc. 2013 Oct;45(10):1965-70. doi: 10.1249/MSS.0b013e318295a9fc. PMID: 24048319

11 The Royal Children's Hospital Melbourne. *Australian Child Health Poll, June 2017*

12 Hardy LL, Merom D, Thomas M, Peralta L. 30-year changes in Australian children's standing broad jump: 1985-2015. J Sci Med Sport. 2018 Oct;21(10):1057-1061. doi: 10.1016/j.jsams.2018.04.005. Epub 2018 May 17. PMID: 29807720

13 https://humankinetics.me/2019/04/12/ltad-model/

14 Oxford Dictionary

15 Collins, H., Booth, J.N., Duncan, A. et al. The effect of resistance training interventions on fundamental movement skills in youth: a meta-analysis. *Sports Med — Open* **5,** 17 (2019). https://doi.org/10.1186/s40798-019-0188-x

16 García-Hermoso, A., Ramírez-Campillo, R. & Izquierdo, M. Is Muscular Fitness Associated with Future Health Benefits in Children and Adolescents? A Systematic Review and Meta-Analysis of Longitudinal Studies. *Sports Med* **49,** 1079–1094 (2019). https://doi.org/10.1007/s40279-019-01098-6

17 Lloyd, Rhodri S. PhD, CSCS*D[1]; Oliver, Jon L. PhD[2] The Youth Physical Development Model: A New Approach to Long-Term Athletic Development, Strength and Conditioning Journal: June 2012 — Volume 34 — Issue 3 — p 61-72 doi: 10.1519/SSC.0b013e31825760ea

18 Adapted from Managing the Training Load in Adolescent Athletes. International Journal of Sports Physiology and Performance, 2017, 12, S2-42 -S2-49. 2017 Human Kinetics, Inc.

19 Bell. Et al. (2018) *Sport specialization and risk of overuse injuries: A systematic review with meta-analysis.*

20 You can access these guidelines at https://www1.health.gov.au/internet/main/publishing.nsf/Content/health-pubhlth-strateg-phys-act-guidelines

21 Duckworth, A (2018). *Grit: The Power of Passion and Perseverance*

22 Stevens, G. Riley, L. & Bull, F. (2019). *Global trends in insufficient physical activity among adolescents: a pooled analysis of 298 population-based surveys with 1·6 million participants.* The Lancet Child & Adolescent Health. 4. 10.1016/S2352-4642(19)30323-2

23 Mitchell Institute for Education and Health Policy, Victoria University (2019). *Sport Participation and Play — How to Get More Australians Moving*

24 Australian Sports Commission (2017). *Australian kids need active sporty parents*

www.ingramcontent.com/pod-product-compliance
Lightning Source LLC
Chambersburg PA
CBHW060521010526
44107CB00060B/2646